# Bullied Kids
# Speak Out

*We Survived—How You Can Too*

## Jodee Blanco

Author of the *New York Times* Bestseller
*Please Stop Laughing at Me . . .*

Avon, Massachusetts

Copyright © 2015 by Jodee Blanco.
All rights reserved.
This book, or parts thereof, may not be reproduced in any form without permission from the publisher; exceptions are made for brief excerpts used in published reviews.

Published by
Adams Media, a division of F+W Media, Inc.
57 Littlefield Street, Avon, MA 02322. U.S.A.
*www.adamsmedia.com*

ISBN 10: 1-4405-7953-9
ISBN 13: 978-1-4405-7953-0
eISBN 10: 1-4405-7954-7
eISBN 13: 978-1-4405-7954-7

Printed in the United States of America.

10   9   8   7   6   5   4   3   2   1

**Library of Congress Cataloging-in-Publication Data**

Blanco, Jodee,
  Bullied kids speak out / Jodee Blanco.
      pages cm
  Includes index.
  Audience: Grade 9 to 12.
    ISBN 978-1-4405-7953-0 (pb) -- ISBN 1-4405-7953-9 (pb) -- ISBN 978-1-4405-7954-7 (ebook) -- ISBN 1-4405-7954-7 (ebook)
  1.  Bullying--Juvenile literature. 2.  Bullying in school--Juvenile literature.  I. Title.
  BF637.B85B568 2015
  302.34'3--dc23

                              2014033507

Many of the designations used by manufacturers and sellers to distinguish their products are claimed as trademarks. Where those designations appear in this book and F+W Media, Inc. was aware of a trademark claim, the designations have been printed with initial capital letters.

The stories detailed in this book are based on actual accounts that have been related to the author by victims of bullying. Names, identifying characteristics, and certain facets of stories have been changed to supply anonymity for all persons involved. Any significant similarities in these stories to actual events is entirely coincidental.

Author photo by Ryan Rossler.
Cover design by Andy Carpenter.
Cover image © iStockphoto.com/LeoGrand.

*This book is available at quantity discounts for bulk purchases.*
*For information, please call 1-800-289-0963.*

## Dedication

*I dedicate this book to my mom, Joy Blanco, who has put up
with me when absolutely no one else would or could, loved me
at my best and my worst, inspired me when I was lost, made me
macaroni and cheese when I was longing for comfort food, taken
care of my dogs, my bunnies, my heart, my soul, and who is the
most important person in my life. I love you, Mom. Thanks for
all the chats.*

*And to*

*My Aunt Anne in heaven, without whom I couldn't write a
word. Not a single word.*
*I love you, too.*

# Contents

# Introduction

Hi. I'm glad you're here! If we've already met, either through one of my other books or perhaps because I've spoken at your school, it's so cool to see you again. And if this is our first time hanging out, I'm happy that we found each other. I want you to know you're safe here, that you're not alone. We all understand what you're going through. When I was in school, I never thought it would get better. I can still hear my classmates laughing at me. I can still feel the sting of all those parties I never got invited to, the football games on Friday nights I longed to attend but didn't dare because I knew I'd be sitting alone in the bleachers, humiliated and ashamed. Don't even get me started about what it was like in the cafeteria at lunch or in the locker room after gym class. Back then there was no Internet. When I got home from school, I was beyond lonely, but at least no one could mess with me in the sanctity of my own home on a computer or smartphone. Cyber-bullying was a monster of the future, one whose claws hadn't yet scratched, whose teeth hadn't yet bitten. Now that monster is unleashed. It's just one more way the mean kids can break your heart. I know all about feeling broken. I also know what it feels like to survive and come back stronger, smarter, and better than before. So do the kids you'll be meeting here. They never gave up. Some took longer than others, and some made a lot of mistakes before getting it right, but every one of them found a way to stand up to their bullies and reclaim their lives. Not only will they give you hope that you can too, but they'll tell you exactly how they did it.

Welcome home. It's time for you to get to know everyone!

# CHAPTER ONE

# Ethan

My mom found me in the barn after school trying to make a noose out of a piece of rope. She grabbed it out of my hands, screaming, "Oh, my God!" over and over. Would I have gone through with it if she hadn't caught me? I don't know. I was desperate. And a few weeks before, I was so happy it was crazy.

I'm sixteen but everyone thinks I'm older 'cause I'm a big dude—not fat but I've got a lot of muscles. I've always struggled to fit in. A few kids at school are okay to me, but I also get made fun of a lot.

There's this girl in my class. Her name is Morgan. I crushed on her since middle school. She's got long blonde hair and awesome green eyes. It took me all semester to get up the nerve to ask her to prom. I'll never forget that day. I was so scared I almost barfed. I went up to her by her locker and just said it.

"Wanna go to prom with me?"

She probably only took like two seconds to answer but it felt like forever. She said, "Okay, sure." It was the best moment of my whole, entire life! I started texting everybody I knew. By second period, a lot of the kids from the cool crowd, who normally looked down on me, were high-fiving me in the halls. Seriously, it was unreal. Usually I felt invisible at school. When I told my parents, they were psyched. They totally got how scary it was asking one of the most popular girls in my class to go with me. I didn't care that she was popular. I would have given anything to take her to prom no matter what. I loved who she was on the inside.

So, like, I really got into planning for this thing. I tried on about a thousand tuxedos to find the coolest one. I Googled a ton of romantic restaurants. I wanted everything to be perfect. I texted my friends with questions. They were like, "Yo, dude, chill." I couldn't help it. I was tripping. My parents were even renting me a limo, and my dad bought a new camera so he could take pictures of Morgan and me all dressed up. My parents had never ridden in a limo in their lives, not even when they got hitched. I knew they really couldn't afford it, but they were so excited for me. I have the best parents on the whole planet.

Then a week before prom, Morgan bailed. She sent me a text that said she couldn't do prom with me 'cause she didn't want to go as someone's "beard." I felt like a total loser 'cause I didn't even know what that meant. I just texted back, "Huh?"

"OMG dude, WTF did you expect after what you posted?" her next message said.

"What post?" I said.

"Seriously?" she said. "Ethan, you like came out to the whole school on FB!"

"I'm not even on FB anymore," I said. "My parents made me get off 'cause my grades sucked."

"Whatever," she said. "You know, I really did like you. You should have told me you were gay. Now I just feel like an idiot."

I kept trying to tell her it wasn't true, that it was some f___ed-up joke. I knew she didn't believe me. She texted me that her friends were all laughing at her. I was used to getting picked on. Morgan wasn't. It freaked her out. Everybody was gossiping about it. It all happened so quick. Everybody started calling me fag and homo. I won't even tell you what some asshole wrote across my locker. The same people who had high-fived me before were trashing me now behind my back. One guy spat in my food at lunch, saying fags shouldn't be allowed to eat with everyone else. I could tell some of the other kids felt bad for me, but they were too scared to say anything. I sat alone in the back of the cafeteria. I could see Morgan at her table with her friends. Some of them were still giving her sh_t. Every once in a while she'd look over at me and then turn away. I never picked on the gay kids at school, but I never stuck up for them. Now I knew exactly how they felt. I wish I had said something when they were getting messed with.

By sixth period, I was so upset that I went to the nurse's office and pretended to be sick so I could go home. When my mom picked me up, she knew something bad happened. That night I told my parents the whole story. Then, we went onto Facebook and found my page. I f___ing lost it. Whoever did it really knew what they were doing. Someone at school must have used their phone to take a picture of me in math class. I knew it was in math, 'cause I recognized the background. I started going through faces in my head, trying to figure out who hated me enough to be so mean. I was so pissed off. My "page" had my favorite movies, favorite music, cool stuff I did last summer on vacation. It was like I wrote it. It even *sounded* like me.

My parents kept calling Facebook but they couldn't get a person on the phone. It was like a nightmare only it was real. My mom called the police, the state's attorney's office, the FBI, our lawyer. Everyone said lots of stuff but no one had an answer. The next morning, she called the principal for a meeting. She said it was an emergency. His secretary treated her like sh_t, told her it was "anti-bullying week," and he was busy trying to get ready for the speaker who was coming, that maybe he could see them next week. Mom was pissed. She and my dad got in the car and drove over there. They told the receptionist all they needed was ten minutes with the principal. She said he was in a meeting with the superintendent but that they could wait if they wanted to. My parents sat in that office for three hours. They finally went home. I've never seen them that mad.

The FB thing wasn't any easier to fix. Finally, after a gazillion e-mails back and forth and a letter from our lawyer, Facebook took down the phony page. By then it didn't matter anymore. Everyone at school still thought I was the one who put it up and that I just wussed out and took it down. Not only was I a "homo," but I was a coward too.

Kids started shoving me into the lockers. This one group of dudes beat me up by the bleachers. Mom asked me about the bruises. I hated having to tell her. And we still didn't know who posted the fake page. The school principal wasn't doing jack. He finally met with my parents and me for twenty minutes, then he sent out a "stern warning" to students about cyber-bullying, and that was that. He said the school couldn't punish whoever made the page anyway, 'cause it happened off school property. I hated my school. Every day it was the same thing. I'd take as much sh_t from the other kids as I could, and then I'd go back to the principal, telling him please, you gotta do something. I like begged the dude. He'd promise me he'd take care of it, and then nada.

I kept on hoping that this would all go away and that Morgan would come around, that she'd still go to prom with me. I couldn't help it. The day of the dance, I wouldn't even go to the bathroom without my cell phone just in case she called or texted to tell me she changed her mind. By six o'clock, reality hit. It was like that amazing moment when I thought my dream had come true, had been just that. A dream. So I snuck into the barn and reached for the rope. That's when Mom found me.

A lot has happened since then.

Mom and Dad convinced me that offing myself wasn't the answer. I can't believe I let things go that far. They told me it *was* time to take control. For months, the school had been talking about the speaker they were bringing in on bullying. We decided to use it as our opportunity. That morning, we showed up at the principal's office, since we knew the speaker would have to check in at the main desk. When the principal came out to meet her, we asked if we could talk to her. We were cool about it, totally respectful. The principal started to say no, but before he could finish, the speaker smiled and put her arm around me. It's like she already got what was going on. Then she said she'd be happy to hear my story. The principal looked like he swallowed a bug. It was awesome! We didn't have much time, since she was scheduled to speak pretty soon. I totally spilled to her. I didn't hold anything back. My parents said some stuff too, but mostly they let me get everything off my chest. I'm not sure if the principal was pretending to give a sh_t or if he really did. Either way, he had to help me. He knew he couldn't dick us around any longer 'cause now there was a witness from outside school. He asked me if it was okay if he told my story at the next school board meeting. He said it might help convince everyone that the "anti-bullying policies" at our school sucked.

I said sure. Then something else happened that was incredible—I still can't believe it really happened. After the speaker finished her talk at my school, she asked to see me. She said a reporter from a big national newspaper called her. She wanted to know if she knew any kids who got bullied and if they'd talk about it. The speaker wanted to know if she could give this reporter my name and number. I was like, "Way cool!" The reporter called that night. We talked, and then she flew out to meet me and my parents. She interviewed my principal too. A couple of weeks later, I couldn't believe it! Our story made the front page of one of the largest newspapers in the country and it was on some national news websites! The writer talked about how stuff really can get done when kids, parents, and the school work together. There was no way my school could wiggle out of doing something now. My principal, who was freaking about the whole thing in the beginning but then finally took a chill pill and did the interview, called to thank me. He told me that I'd "taught him a valuable lesson about integrity and standing up for what's right even when you're afraid."

Today, the new rules at my school are way better than before, and if a student is being bullied, there's what they call "an accountability process." If a teacher doesn't help they get in trouble. Finally, kids like me have a chance.

*Ethan, you and your parents should be proud of yourselves for never giving up. I'm relieved they were able to help you understand that suicide is never the answer. Your life matters.*

*For everyone who's listening today, if you ever feel like Ethan did and you're thinking about taking your own life, stop, right now, and listen to me. You never know what tomorrow will bring. Look what happened with Ethan! He found the strength to keep on going and you can too. He not only made things better at his high school; he gave hope to each person who read about his story in the newspaper. If you're struggling like Ethan was at first, turn to an adult you trust, whether it's one of your parents, the parent of a friend, or someone at school, and ask for support and guidance.*

*When it comes to reporting bullying, keep in mind that every school is different. If you tell your counselor you're being bullied and the situation doesn't improve, don't just give up. Take it up the chain of command. Next, talk to the principal. If that doesn't work, go to the superintendent. If you're still not seeing results, ask your parents to take you to the next school board meeting and tell your story. Type it up beforehand, and have copies with you ready to hand out. Documentation is a persuasive tool. If that doesn't yield results, and you know you've done everything you can, that you've made a sincere effort to work with the school, reach out to the education writer at your local paper and engage the power of the press.*

*Above all, stay strong, keep your cool, and persevere.*

# CHAPTER TWO

# Taylor

My life was falling apart. It all started 'cause I couldn't stand watching my friends constantly pick on this poor girl in my class. Her name was Amy. She was super shy and couldn't look at anyone. She could have been really pretty if she wanted, but she never took care of herself by the way she looked. She was invisible. I said to my friends that we should invite her to one of our amazing Friday sleepovers, and give her a makeover. My BFF, Alexis, got pissed.

"What is *wrong* with you?" she said. "Amy's a total freak!"

"Why do you always have to be so mean?" I said. "Maybe if somebody at this school gave her a chance she'd be a whole different person."

I felt bad for Amy. Every day at lunch, she'd sit by herself. Sometimes, I'd catch her staring at our table. She wanted to sit with us. I said to my friends, "Come on you guys, let's at least invite her to sit with us."

They all laughed.

My friends and I were part of the popular clique. We were varsity cheerleaders. We got good grades and dated the hottest guys at school. My boyfriend was on the basketball team and debate. I always had tons of cool stuff to do with my friends. I just thought that was normal. I was stressed out about applying to colleges, but everyone in my group was too, so it was just one more thing we could bond over when we hung out.

Amy had gone to school with us since sixth grade. She was always made fun of a little but none of us paid much attention 'cause we were used to it, and besides, she never said anything. Some kids got picked on, and she was one of them. It's just how it was. But that year, things got really twisted. The other kids started messing with Amy's head. It's like they wanted to break her, to see her melt down. This jerk in my math class asked Amy for a date, and then, he stood her up. When she sent him a text the next day at school asking why he never even called, he said, "Holy sh_t, baby, you didn't think I was *serious*! Why would anyone go out with a dog like you? Arf! Arf!" When he saw her in the hallway, he was with a bunch of his friends and they all started barking at her. I wasn't there, but one of them told me about it. He was smiling, thought it was hilarious. I heard from the nurse Amy was so upset that she barfed and had to go home early.

It made me sick. Even my BFFs were getting into it. Everyone was on Facebook and Pinterest and Twitter. They'd trash-talk Amy and any other kids they looked down on too. My classmates were becoming meaner all the time. I felt like I was in some horror movie, and one by one, all my friends were being taken over by evil beings, sent here to destroy the earth, or at least our school. Finally, I had to pick a side.

After gym class I was in the locker room changing. Alexis started pushing Amy around, calling her names I don't even want to say here. Amy kept asking her to stop, but the more she begged, the harder Alexis tried to hurt her. Everyone knew Amy's mom was a little off. Amy had to live with her grandma for six months the year before, 'cause her mom had been in the hospital for "exhaustion," which we all knew was code for some sort of breakdown.

"Amy, the moment your mom got pregnant with you, she should have committed suicide," Alexis told her.

I was shocked. I couldn't believe what had just come out of my best friend's mouth. Amy just stood there, shaking. I ran over to her and hugged her. She told me her mom did try to kill herself, she swallowed a bottle of pills, and that's why she was in the hospital last year. I told myself Alexis couldn't have known that. By now, Amy was crying and I was trying to comfort her. Alexis was giving me one of her famous dirty looks. I was starting to figure out that my BFF was a royal bitch.

"Why do you even care about that worthless chick?" she said. "Since when do you give a sh_t about anyone but you?"

Just then the bell rang, thank God. I walked Amy to the nurse's office and told her to chill there for a while.

"Thanks," she said. "I didn't mean to get you into trouble with your friend."

"That's okay," I said. "With friends like that, who needs enemies?" We both laughed.

Cheerleading practice was a nightmare. Alexis turned the whole squad against me. It sucked. All I did was help someone who needed a friend. Why do you only get to choose friends who your other friends are cool with, and if you want to be friends with someone they don't like, you're screwed? It's not fair. Every day, things got worse. My BFFs started tripping me during practice. For one of our routines we had to form a pyramid. As we were getting into position, someone whispered, "I hope you break your neck, bitch." There was so much hate in her voice, it was like *dripping* with it. I couldn't take it. I ran out of the gym. The coach came after me and said she thought I should take some time off, that I was a "distraction to the others." I guess Alexis got to her too . . .

My friends didn't like me hanging with someone they didn't think was cool and they were going to make me pay for it until I stopped. Alexis, and even my boyfriend, only seemed to care about me when I was doing what they wanted. I couldn't be my own person, and when I finally did something for someone other than myself, when I acted unselfishly for once, everybody started hating on me.

For a week, I kept trying to figure out what to do next. I didn't tell my mom about having to take time off from cheerleading. Instead, when I was supposed to be at practice, I went to the movies or hung out at the mall instead. My mom was clueless about the whole thing until one of the other cheerleader's moms called to say how sorry she was about what happened. I knew when I got home and saw my mom's face that I'd have to tell the truth. So I did. I told her how mean my friends were acting this year, how Alexis messed with Amy for no reason, and how I couldn't handle it anymore, that even if it meant losing all my friends, better that than losing myself. I thought she'd freak because she'd always been so proud of her "popular daughter." She was bullied in high school, and seeing me hanging out with the "in-crowd" took away some of that pain. It was like justice for her. Now, I wasn't only unpopular; I was a target.

"I'm so glad you reached out to Amy," Mom said. "I've never been prouder of you."

I couldn't believe my ears. My mom surprised me. I thought she'd be mad at me for blowing everything.

"I feel terrible you were afraid to confide in me, that you had to go through this alone," she said. "Promise me that will never, ever happen again, that you'll always talk to me, no matter what, okay?"

That night, when my dad got home from work, Mom and I told him the entire story. He listened to every word, and then, together, we came up with a plan. I couldn't wait!

First, I made a list of all the kids at school who were being bullied; Amy wasn't the only one. Then, I called Amy and asked her if she wanted to start an anti-bullying club with me. At first she wasn't very into it, but I convinced her. We went to the principal together. It was a hard meeting because I had to tell him what happened with Alexis. He asked me if she'd been behaving like this for a while. I told him she could be bitchy sometimes, but lately, it was way over the top. I thought he'd want to punish her, but he was worried about her. It made me feel bad that I hadn't been worried about her too. After all, we had been best friends since middle school. I decided that that would be one of the goals of our club, to not just give bullied students somewhere to turn for support, but to help the bullies, too.

The principal was psyched about the club idea, and he said he could even find some money for it. Amy and I began signing up members. Some kids were totally into being asked (the fact I had been popular was working for me in a way I never imagined). Others didn't want to be in a club for "freaks and losers," but when we explained what we had planned, like makeover parties, inviting their favorite authors to come and speak at the school, meeting with politicians about bullying, and other really cool things, they got more interested. It wasn't easy, but within a month, we were the talk of the school! Our first official meeting, the superintendent and the town mayor did a proclamation in our honor, launching the club.

Slowly, some of my old friends, who had sided with Alexis, told me they were sorry and that they'd like to get into the club. We worked with the school counselor on a Students Bill of Rights that said what to do if you're bullied and what to expect back from the school. It created "accountability," which my dad told me was a big deal.

I'll always be grateful to the principal for teaching me that having compassion for the bully, and trying to find out what's wrong, is more important than punishment. It finally came out that Alexis was in an awful situation at home. She never told me. She'd never told any of us, but her dad had tried to kill himself. No wonder she made that nasty crack to Amy. She was in her own hell and taking it out on everyone and everything.

If you're going through what I did and feel like your friends are all turning on you, even though it's scary, you have to be true to your own heart. Speak up for people who won't defend themselves or can't. I think it's more important to like yourself than to have others think you're cool. I know it may not seem like that now, but try it. Follow that little voice inside you that you know is telling you the right thing to do. See what happens. You'll be totally relieved that you did.

*Taylor, I'm so proud of your strength! Even more importantly, I'm proud of your compassion. If anyone here is going through what Taylor did, I know how scary it is, but you're braver than you think. Don't let the fear of losing your friends make you less than who you are. Your real friends will support you. One thing Taylor learned from this experience is the real meaning of friendship. Friends are not people who only care about you when you live up to their concept of cool. Taylor couldn't be her own person if she allowed others to dictate to her who she should be. She—and you—can do things not just for yourselves but for others. Your real friends will support you. Even if they don't right away, they'll come around eventually. Those who turn on you completely were never friends to begin with, and deep down you know that.*

*If you know someone who's being meaner than usual, who's acting in ways she never did before, instead of becoming angry or wanting to get back at that person for hurting you, be curious. Try to find out as much as you can about what's happening in that person's life. Ask anyone who might be able to offer information. Chances are, like Alexis, you'll discover the bully is going through something he hasn't told you about, and he's bringing all that unresolved fear and anger to school. Curiosity leads to compassion. The more you know about the bully's story, the more you'll be able to help everyone involved.*

*Curiosity is also important when it comes to helping those who are being bullied. Think about all the kids at your school who get picked on or maybe just feel invisible. Make a list like Taylor did, and reach out to them. Ask around. Make sure you* haven't overlooked anyone. I'm an activist. That means I take action to motivate action in others. Taylor became an activist the moment she defended Amy. You can be an activist too. Start an anti-bullying club at your school. You may feel alone, but you're not. You CAN make a difference.

Lastly, Taylor was afraid to tell her mom what was going on at first. And when she finally did tell the truth, her mom was totally supportive. She was afraid and didn't have to be. Unless you have a really bad relationship with your parents, trust them. Talk to them. Let them in. They may surprise you like Taylor's mom surprised her. If you and your parents aren't on good terms, before you decide not to tell them anything, talk it out with your school counselor or another adult you trust. Ask them if they would help you break the ice. Sometimes, all it takes is another adult to smooth things over.

# CHAPTER THREE

# Cameron

Zero tolerance policies suck. This jerk in my math class, Tyler, who'd been on me since the beginning of the year, got so up in my face one afternoon I could smell the peanut butter on his breath from lunch. He pinned me against the locker and kept saying what a pussy I was. His friends laughed and told him to kick the sh_t out of me.

I wasn't afraid to fight. I didn't want to get hurt and blow my chances of a dance scholarship. All I ever wanted was to be a dancer. I went straight from school to dance practice. I'd been taking dance lessons since I was little. My mom was raising me alone and we never had enough money. A scholarship was my only shot at my dream and I wasn't about to risk it on some stupid fight.

I was in eighth grade, but I worried about stuff way more than other kids my age. My mom said I was an "old soul." My dad left us when I was a baby. I barely remember him. It was just my mom, my sister, and me. Everybody at school thought I was weird, and they told me all the time that I'd never fit in. Gym class was rough. I hated dodge ball most. Some of the kids threw the ball at my face. They got in trouble a few times, but it only made things worse. My doctor, who was a friend of my mom's, said he'd write me a note to get me excused from PE, but my school had a rule that if you couldn't participate, you still had to change into your gym uniform and cheer on the other kids from the bleachers. Something about "team spirit." What a choice—they were friggin' going to make fun of me either way. I toughed it out.

Every day, I hated school more. I was sick of being looked down on. Tyler and his friends wouldn't give me a break. They made fun of how I dressed, my hair, my voice. Anything. I was into old clothes and wore lots of cool hats. I had this awesome black fedora, like the ones in black-and-white movies, and I'd wear it with an old tweed blazer and jeans. It was a cool look, and I liked looking cool. Mom let me make some of my own clothes. I did tons of stuff with bright colors, and made stuff with unusual patterns and designs. I made all my own dance costumes too. Part of it was because I loved doing it. Part of it was also about money. We lived in a town in New York where almost everyone at school came from serious money. My mom worked two jobs, and while we didn't want for anything, we couldn't afford Abercrombie either. We were always on a budget. I know I could have tried to look more like everybody else, but it made me mad that I had to be less than who I was to be accepted. Besides, I did it in sixth grade and it was a disaster. My classmates knew I was trying to be someone I wasn't, and they made fun of me more. I decided it was better to be true to myself even if they didn't like it.

That day Tyler messed with me by the lockers, I knew he wanted to start a fight. He didn't care about getting into trouble. That would only make him look cooler to his friends. I thought I was going to throw up from his breath.

"Come on, dude, just friggin' get off me," I said.

"What a pussy!"

"Cut it out!" I said.

He and his friends kept laughing.

I tried to push him away.

Just then, a teacher came running over. We were both sent to the principal's office and suspended for three days for fighting. When I told my mom, she was furious at my principal.

"Why should *you* get suspended too?" she said. "You're the victim here!"

"I know, Mom, but that's how the school is," I told her. "It's zero tolerance."

"I understand that, but what else could you have done? Tyler had you pinned down. All you were trying to do was break free."

Mom wanted to stand up to them. She didn't have it easy where we lived either. Most of the other parents were snobs. Mom told me when she went to PTA meetings the other people looked at her like she didn't belong, but it never stopped her from being heard. My mom had a lot of balls. When this stuff with Tyler happened, she decided to change things herself. She asked authors and experts to come to the school and speak. She called lawyers. Some of them helped her for free. I was proud of her, but a part of me was freaking out too. The principal and some of the other parents were getting really pissed off, and I already had it hard enough at school.

After my suspension was over, I didn't have any friends. Tyler's dad grounded him over the suspension, and he blamed me. Tyler was popular, and if you stood up to him or anyone in that clique, you'd pay for it. Between that and my mom's stuff, no one wanted to hang out with me. I kept dancing and tried to ignore the bullies. That's what a lot of adults tell you to do. *It never works.* I learned the hard way that year. The more I ignored them—you should have seen the sick things they posted on YouTube. The more I tried not to pay attention to them, the meaner they got. When they started tripping me in the halls, and going after my knees in dodge ball, I couldn't take it anymore . . .

My dance coach set me straight. She said I needed to get my confidence back. She told me that I never hung out with the kids from dance class, that I had become too much of a loner. The other kids thought I was stuck-up. That really bothered me. I wasn't stuck-up. I was afraid if they really got to know me outside of dance practice, they wouldn't like me. My confidence sucked. So I did what she said. I started talking to other kids in dance. We began hanging out a lot. There were way more girls than guys, and I'd never thought about it before, but that was pretty cool. My coach was right. Within weeks, I felt way better about myself. And you want to know the best part? The more I got into my new friends, the less I cared whether people at school liked me. When I stopped caring, the people at school did start to come around. It was so weird. Like at lunch, some of my old friends who had been totally ignoring me since the Tyler thing started talking to me again. They even asked me to sit with them at lunch. I still got bullied in gym class, but then my dance coach gave me this great idea. Part of gym class was square-dancing, but everyone hated it. It was totally lame and no one did it anymore in real life. So I asked my gym teacher if we could do hip-hop instead. At first he wasn't sure, but when I told some of the other kids in my class about the idea, they were so into it that we convinced our teacher. Since he didn't know hip-hop himself, I volunteered to teach everyone the basic moves. I even said we should do a hip-hop contest, where kids could make up their own steps and get extra credit. Gym went from being the worst part of my school day to the best. Some of the other kids still give me a hard time, but at least now, I don't feel so alone every day. People stick up for me, when before that would never happen.

I also started being nicer to my mom. I had been a real jerk to her since she started taking on the administration. She was doing it for me and I should be trying to help. I asked her what was going on, and she told me she was making prog-ress. The superintendent was doing a special teacher meeting on bullying and invited Mom. She was shocked when I told her I wanted to be there too to support her. The day of the meeting, the superintendent thanked my mom for all she was doing for the district and then he asked her to give a speech. I was so proud. Who knew my mom could be such a good speaker! She was totally chill and super persuasive. She had tons of statistics about bullying, and why zero tolerance can be unfair. I saw a lot of teachers nodding their heads and taking notes. When she was finished, everyone clapped. Even the principal was smiling.

*Cameron, I am so proud of both you and your mom, I could burst into applause myself! It took a lot of character to do what you guys did. Not only were you able to impact the adults in the school, but you had an effect on students, too. And I know the*

*guts it took to put yourself out there with your dance mates. Your classmates had already burned you, and the possibility of rejection and ridicule again must have been terrifying. But you faced your fears, and look at the results!*

*One very important lesson to learn from Cameron's experience: If you're being bullied, I don't care what your parents or counselor has told you. DO NOT ignore the bullies. I repeat, DO NOT ignore them! I'll never understand why adults say that to bullied kids. First they tell you, "Don't be a bystander; if someone is getting bullied, defend that person," but then they'll turn around and say to you in the same breath, "Oh, you're being bullied? Just ignore it and walk away." Isn't that a mixed message? Aren't all those adults asking you to be a bystander in your own life? What they're suggesting is harmful. Then those same adults wonder why kids constantly tell them they don't understand. They don't. When you ignore the bullies, all you do is give them permission to keep on messing with you. Stand up for yourself. No one has the right to hurt you.*

*For those of you who are dealing with a similar situation to the one in which Cameron found himself, I understand how scary the thought of making new friends can be. Sometimes you have to go beyond your comfort zone and take a risk. The rewards can be great, and not doing anything, staying locked inside your own head, frustrated that nothing is changing in your life, but too scared to do what's necessary to change it, doesn't work either. If you're not involved in any activities outside of school, start doing some research. Ask your parents or counselor to help you. Google the park district, local public library, and community center the next town over from where you live and see what they offer for kids. It's important to get far enough away from your school that you'll meet all new people. Most of these organizations feature everything from dance, martial arts, and soccer, to theater and crafts. You can also search activities and clubs for teens. There are private dance studios, music and drama clubs, the list goes on and on. Find something you think might be cool and enroll. It'll give you something to look forward to and a whole new group of friends. Sometimes, when a person wants to fit in at school, he can try too hard, and it has the opposite effect. When you've got a social life somewhere else, you'll be more relaxed and feel better about yourself. Having a new vibe can make all the difference with your classmates.*

*Look how far Cameron and his mom came in just a few months. As you can see from their experience, there are many ways to stand up to bullies. Cameron didn't have to use his fists. Instead he used his humanity and his talents. Meanwhile, his mom put her courage to work. They're both heroes!*

*Before I sign off, I want to offer one more piece of advice. You know how Cameron wants to be a professional dancer? That's so cool that he has that dream. If you have a dream like Cameron of what you want to be when you're older, don't wait until college to get started. Get moving right now! For example, if you want to be a dancer like Cameron, dedicate one hour a day to your goal. Research your favorite dancers and how they achieved success. Where did they go to school? What did they major in? Who's their agent? How did they get their big break? What you learn could help you accomplish your own dreams. And most of all, never give up. Keep striving every day.*

## CHAPTER FOUR

# Brianna

Hi. I'm Brianna. I'm in seventh grade. Earlier this year, something awful happened at school. My teacher, Ms. Beals, had to move to another state 'cause of her husband's job, and I got this new teacher, Mr. Jenson. He taught at another school and was supposed to retire.

I loved Ms. Beals. She was the only person I could talk to about stuff. I'm an only child and my parents treated me like a grownup. They yelled at me if I acted immature. I didn't fit in at school. Ms. Beals was nice to me. She never judged me. On really bad days, she'd find a way to make me smile. I know it's weird to say this about a teacher, but Ms. Beals was my BFF.

I go to a private school and we have only one teacher all the way through. It's a creative school. I love being creative. The only problem was that most of the kids knew each other since kindergarten and I didn't start till way later. I'd get invited to stuff, and once in a while someone would ask me to hang out, but I didn't really think they liked me. This girl Kayla is really popular. Her parents gave a ton of money to the school, and her mom is on the board. Kayla and her friends wouldn't give me a chance. They told me I would never belong. I tried to talk to them. They made fun of me more. I tried going along with them, and they joked about how pathetic I was. If I said something smart to them, they'd mock me.

Nothing, nothing, *nothing* worked.

I had cancer up until fifth grade. Nobody except my parents and the doctors and the teachers knew. I didn't want the kids at school to know. I thought they'd feel weird around me. Cancer freaks out a lot of people, like they're nervous it's contagious or something. My parents told me I should be honest about it but they didn't push me.

My mom homeschooled me while I was sick. I didn't go to a real school until last year. I didn't really know how to relate to kids my own age except the ones I got to know in the hospital. When I started at the academy, I felt like an alien. If it wasn't for Ms. Beals, I would have wanted homeschooling again. I tried to talk to Mr. Jenson about it. I went to his office and poured my heart out. He just looked at the papers he was grading and ignored me. He wasn't nice in class either. During English one day, he asked if anyone could recite a poem we were supposed to have memorized. This shy boy, who never liked to be called on, raised his hand. He got halfway through the poem, but he couldn't remember the last part.

"Next time, young man, you'd best be sure of yourself before you waste this classroom's time," Mr. Jenson said.

I felt so bad for this kid. Half the class looked at one another, like, we couldn't believe what we had just seen. He hasn't raised his hand since. Mr. Jenson wanted his students to be scared of him. In the middle of social studies one afternoon, I felt really tired and put my head down. Mr. Jenson stopped the class, came over to my desk, and said, "Brianna, if you want to take a nap, I suggest you go to the nurse's office." Everybody started laughing. I felt ashamed. If I needed to rest during the school day, the teachers were supposed to hand me a nurse's pass and not make a big thing out of it, and later, I'd get whatever work I'd missed. Mr. Jenson didn't care. A lot of parents were complaining about Mr. Jenson. The principal knew they didn't like him, but she was having a hard time finding someone else. I was so upset I started getting colds and sore throats every other week. Then I found out that this girl I knew from the hospital died. I cried all day. I wished it had been me instead of her. She was so cool. She loved animals and said that one day she was going to start an animal rescue place. It was so unfair. I was miserable. She should have lived.

The next day, when I went to school, I decided I was going to do something in her honor. I didn't know what or how. I just knew I had to do something. I asked God to help me. It was social studies class. Mr. Jenson told us to open our books to chapter five. He asked us if we'd done the home-work assignment, which was to have read the chapter and be ready to answer questions. We all nodded. Suddenly, we heard somebody's phone ping. Cell phones were supposed to be turned off during class. Mr. Jenson got really mad. He walked around the room asking us to put our cell phones on our desks. Everyone's was off except Kayla's.

"Young lady, principal's office, *now!*" he yelled.

"I'm sorry, Mr. Jenson," she said. "My dog was really sick this morning and my mom was just texting me from the vet that he'll be okay."

"Now!"

"Please, Mr. Jenson, I'm sorry."

He wouldn't let up. Kayla had been mean to me all year, but she didn't deserve to be put down like that by a teacher.

"Mr. Jenson, you're the one who's disrupting," I said. "Kayla didn't do anything wrong. She was worried about her pet. You're cruel!"

He said, "Brianna, you're treading on very thin ice here."

I shut up. But I knew I wouldn't stay quiet . . .

Later that day Kayla came up to me by the entrance to the cafeteria.

"Hey, you want to sit at our table today?"

I couldn't believe it. I'd never been asked to sit at the popular table before.

"Really?" I said.

"Yeah," she said. "That was so cool what you did today, sticking up for me in Mr. Jenson's class. I hate him. He's so mean."

"I know, it's like he doesn't like kids," I said. "And yeah, I'd love to sit with you guys. That would be awesome."

Finally since I started at the academy, I felt a little hope. Lunch was fun. Kayla and her friends were nice to me. And I wasn't nervous. I was relaxed and chill. I was being myself, and it was okay.

"Hey, Brianna, can I ask you something?" Kayla said. "How come you're not like this all the time? I mean, you're so cool right now, but before when we tried to hang out with you, you were different."

"What do you mean?" I asked.

"It's like you were trying to show off how grown-up you were," Kayla said.

I didn't know what to say.

"You were so serious and intense about stuff."

"I get why you guys would think that," I said. Then I told Kayla and her friends about my cancer. I never thought I'd have the courage to do that. After I was done, they asked me some questions. I answered all of them, even the embarrassing ones.

"You're the bravest person I've ever met in my whole life," Kayla said. "Mr. Jenson better think twice before he messes with you again!" We all laughed.

"No, seriously," Kayla said. "You're not afraid of him like everybody else. You stood up to him. What if we all did, too, like a team on one of those reality shows, and you could be captain!"

That's how it started. We called ourselves Team Finley in honor of Kayla's dog, Finley. If it wasn't for him having to go to the vet, who knows what might have happened with Mr. Jenson?

When I got home from school, I told my parents about the unreal day I'd had and what Kayla and her friends and I were doing. My mom was uncomfortable at first because she didn't want Mr. Jenson freaking out and making our lives worse, but my dad was way cool with it. He convinced her that it would be good for me and help prepare me for the "obstacles of the business world." I know, I know, don't even go there, but if it got Mom on board, fine. That night after dinner, Dad worked with me on a "plan of action." Two days later, I had a sleepover (my first ever—it was *amazing*!) for everyone on the team and we got busy.

Here's what we did and how it all turned out. We made a list of all the kids at school we'd seen Mr. Jenson acting mean to. Then, we wrote a report that had the name of each student and all the details. Next, we printed it out and we got all the students who were in it to read the part about themselves and sign it. Some of them asked us to make changes, which we did. We didn't push any student to sign the report until they were okay with it. After the report was done and everyone had signed, we gave it to our parents to read. Then Kayla's mom called all the members of the school board of trustees, and the principal, and asked for a meeting. She also called and invited all the parents whose kids had Mr. Jenson.

The afternoon of the meeting, we were totally ready. Kayla's mom said some stuff, and then she called on us kids. Each of us read a part of the report. Some students read the part they'd signed. You could tell by the shocked look on some of the parents' faces they had no idea Mr. Jenson had been treating their kids that way. Then, we handed everyone a printed copy of the report. After the meeting, the principal thanked us and told our parents that they should be proud of our courage. She said that she'd talk to Mr. Jenson, and that until this whole thing was fixed, she'd get someone else to teach his classes. It took about a week before we got the letter. It was from Mr. Jenson. Here, I'll let you read it.

Dearest students and parents,

It is with deep regret that I am resigning from the academy to begin my retirement. I'm a forty-year veteran of the military school system, and in striving to uphold those traditions, I failed to honor the most fundamental requirement of teaching: compassion. They say one cannot teach an old dog new tricks, but all of you have taught this old dog that sometimes, patience is more prudent than discipline, understanding more productive than toughness. The old paradigm of "drop down and give me twenty" doesn't work with vulnerable young kids.

I leave here having been humbled, and for that I am grateful. I needed humbling.

I hope that one day some of you will think of me kindly and realize that whatever mistakes I made, they were not out of malice.

Respectfully and sincerely,

Sgt. John S. Jenson

Everybody was blown away. He wasn't a bad person. Mr. Jenson came from a place where being strict was the most important thing. He thought that if any of his students were weak, it was his job to toughen them up, or they'd never survive. He was trying to be tough with everyone, the same way I was always trying so hard to be mature. I never thought about how it must have made the other kids feel, just like Mr. Jenson never thought about how what he was doing made *us* feel. When you get used to being a certain way, you don't always notice how it affects other people. When Kayla told me how the other kids at school saw me, a huge light bulb went on in my head. I was more mature 'cause of everything I went through when I was little, but that didn't mean I couldn't have fun and be silly sometimes. The kids at school didn't hate me; they just didn't understand me, and I made it harder 'cause I didn't try to understand *them*. That's what happened with Mr. Jenson too.

A few days after we got Mr. Jenson's letter, all of us kids got together and we wrote him a note, wishing him luck in his retirement. And we sent him a gift. We made him a big poster with cool quotes from famous military figures (our principal helped) and we all signed it.

*Brianna, I'm proud of you for being strong in a tough situation. Most people think of bullying as kids being mean to other kids. But teachers can be bullies too. For any of you who may be dealing with a teacher bully, don't be afraid to take a stand like Brianna. First, tell your mom and dad and ask for their support. Next, reach out to other classmates who are also struggling with that teacher. Work as a team. Put together a report. Write down every time the teacher bullied someone and give as many details as possible. Be respectful though. Stick to the facts and don't insult the teacher in the report. Simply have each student who was bullied describe what happened in a few sentences, when it happened, and how it made them feel.*

*Once you have everything written down, give it to a parent to review. Then, present it to the principal. And keep in mind that if a teacher is being mean, it's rarely because that teacher doesn't like you. Mr. Jenson didn't dislike Brianna or Kayla, or that boy who raised his hand and then couldn't remember the poem. He thought he was helping them. He didn't realize his method had the opposite effect. Teachers are human too.*

*Have you ever gone through a personal crisis, something really hard, and you took it out on everyone at school? That can happen to teachers too. That's why it's important that when you finally do approach your principal, you approach the situation with respect and compassion.*

*If you need help, let me know. I'm here.*

# CHAPTER FIVE

## Zach

I'm Zach. I'm in eighth grade. I want to be a movie director when I'm older. My dad gave me this really cool video camera, and whenever I'm freaked out about something, I write a scene about it and then make mini-movies. It's how I deal with stuff. I've made tons of mini-movies, and I'm hoping they get me into NYU or UCLA one day. My dream is to make horror movies. They're my favorite.

My story is epic. It started in sixth grade. I kept it to myself for a long time, didn't tell my parents or anyone about what was going on . . .

*Cut* (that's what directors say) *to sixth grade—*

I locked myself in my bedroom and pushed my desk against the door. My mom begged me to come out. I didn't want to talk. It didn't help. Nothing helped. These two dudes on the basketball team, Christian and Dylan, wouldn't stop. Dylan reminded me of that vampire from the Twilight movies, except he wasn't a hero. He was always getting into trouble. Christian thought Dylan was God. What really sucked was that Christian and I used to be friends, but when he started hanging out with Dylan, he became a whole different person.

Every day before science class, I'd see them coming. Dylan would punch my left arm as hard as he could, and then make Christian punch my right one. I could tell Christian didn't want to, but Dylan would make him do it. He'd make fun of Christian and call him terrible names if he didn't. Then, Dylan would bet Christian over who would leave the bigger bruise. The next day, they'd grab me and pull up my sleeves to see who won the bet. The winner got to pick what they would do to me next. It was like a cruelty contest. Sometimes, they'd corner me after homeroom, and one of them would hold on to me while the other stomped on my foot as hard as he could until I cried. I kept hoping some adult would see this stuff going on, but our school was big, and the hallways were total chaos during period changes. You could do almost anything. Unless it got reported, you'd get away with it.

Some of the other guys on the basketball team started throwing garbage at me after lunch. I went to the nurse's office a couple of times to clean up, but I never told her how I got the garbage all over me. I made up dumb excuses because I was afraid if I told, it would get worse. Finally, she figured it out on her own. I asked her not to say anything to the principal but she said she had to because of "school policy."

I said to her, "You're going to ruin my life!"

She said, "If those boys are hurting you, they're likely hurting other students too, and I wouldn't be doing my job if I allowed their behavior to continue."

She called the principal and told him everything. Then she noticed the bruises on my arm and told the principal about that too. He called the bullies into his office. They got in big trouble. Soon, I had a new nickname . . . "Zach the rat."

It sucked. Whenever I went to an adult for help, things always, *always* got worse.

*Cut to later that afternoon—*

I was on the school bus on my way home. I got a text. I thought it was my parents. When I read it, I started to lose the grilled cheese I ate at lunch . . .

It said, "Nowhere is safe now FAT PIG!"

*Close-up of note, intense music plays, scene ends—*

*Cut to the next morning—*

So I sat there in my bedroom, listening to my parents freaking out on the other side of the door, and I didn't care. They sounded like the adults in those Charlie Brown Christmas cartoons: "*Wah, wah, wah.*" They could freak out all they wanted. No way was I ever going to school again. *Ever.*

I stayed in my room that whole day, until I got so hungry I had to go downstairs to eat. I was in hell.

*Fade to black—*

I hadn't always been fat. Up until sixth grade I did tons of sports. I was on the basketball team with Christian and Dylan. I played soccer, and during the summers, my parents sent me to baseball camp. I loved sports and I had tons of friends. But in sixth grade, it's like someone gave them mean pills. They began putting down anyone different from them, when before they never did that.

I love animals, and I don't like to kill anything, not even bugs. There was this huge grasshopper outside by the school buses one day and I was afraid it would get run over, so I picked it up and put it in the bushes. I did things like that all the time. No one ever made a big deal out of it before. Back in fifth grade, we had a mouse problem at school, and the janitor was going to use mousetraps. I thought that was cruel. I couldn't stand it. So my parents helped me raise money to get humane traps. They're really cool. They're these little cages with hearts on them. You put food in the cages and water, and check them twice a day. When a mouse goes inside to eat the cheese (we put cheese in them), the door to the cage automatically closes, and then you take the mouse and let him go outside. We caught all the mice, and my parents and I took them to a field near school. My science teacher gave me extra credit for it, and we did a whole class on animal rights. The other kids thought it was cool.

Then in sixth grade I started getting made fun of for that kind of stuff. It was an epic shock because up until then the other kids looked up to me because I was different. I was kind of the leader. I couldn't understand why all of the sudden they didn't want anything to do with me anymore.

Every day, school sucked more.

So I started to eat.

By the end of sixth grade, I was too out of shape for summer baseball camp. My parents tried to get me into other stuff like horseback riding, swimming, tennis, and even golf (yuck). But I just couldn't get into anything. By the beginning of seventh grade, I was the heaviest kid in my class.

Mom said I was trying to find comfort through food, but the fatter I got, the more I got made fun of. My parents talked to the principal a ton of times, and they even met with Christian's and Dylan's parents. It was a disaster. Everyone blamed everyone else.

I kept eating.

By Christmas break, I began locking myself in my room again, but this time, I stashed food in a cooler in the closet. No way was anyone getting me out of there. I'd rather die alone in my room than face school. My dad had to hire a locksmith to get inside my room. It didn't matter. My parents couldn't make me go to school. They tried once. I screamed so loud, someone called the police. It took an hour for my dad to explain to the cops what was going on, that I wasn't an abused child. But I was not going to school. Every time the bell rang and we had to change periods, I was scared I'd get hit. I didn't want to hear the awful names everyone called me. So finally, my parents gave up. My mom decided to homeschool me for the rest of seventh grade, but eighth grade, I'd have to go back to school, and I could transfer to a new one if I wanted.

The whole homeschooling thing was different than I thought it would be. My parents were like, "No way are you going to stay cooped up all day in the house." If my mom was doing history with me, she'd take me to the museum for the lesson. I didn't think of it at the time, but my mom put her whole life on hold to help me that semester. She also made me work with a trainer and somebody who helped with my diet. My parents were both pretty fit and they wanted me to learn about food and health. They said I could be a normal weight if I tried.

That year, I totally rocked. I studied really hard so I wouldn't be behind when I went back to school. The trainer my parents got me was awesome. He trained a bunch of kids, and twice a week he'd let us work out together. It was fun, and I made friends with the other kids in the group. By the time summer came, I lost almost all the weight I'd gained, and I was hanging out with my new friends from the training group. I could tell my parents were relieved. When it came time for the "big talk," about where I'd go to eighth grade, I decided to go back to my old school. I was afraid but I didn't want to run away.

The first day of school, I called my new friends and they gave me this epic pep talk. By the time I got on the bus, I was psyched. Some of the kids on the bus made fun of me, but I was totally chill. Before I'd have gotten so pissed off I'd want to punch something. This time, I just looked at the bullies and told them off. They were shocked. Then, when I got to school, a bunch of kids came up to me and told me how cool it was that I'd lost so much weight. Even Christian said so. Some kids like Dylan were still jerks and they'd always be jerks. I know now that school will never be perfect, and that in life, not everyone will like you. Some people just suck, period. But I've got my own group of friends and it's cool, and I've also got my workout friends. It's all good.

*Fade to credits.*

*Zach, you've got a lot of character. That means you're strong on the inside and when life is extra hard, you find the courage to keep going and grow from the experience. I'm so very proud of you.*

*If there's anyone listening who's struggling like Zach was, and you're freaking out because you're scared it's never going to get better, it did for Zach and it can for you too. I know sometimes that when life really sucks, it's easy to gain weight, and the more you lose control of what you're eating, the worse you feel. A lot of us have been there.*

*Change is possible, but sometimes it takes a time-out to refocus. When parents ask me about homeschooling, I usually say that I don't think it's a good idea, because the real world doesn't work that way. You have to interact with other people your whole* life and learning how to survive school and find your own path helps prepare you for the challenges of being an adult. In Zach's case, though, I saw the wisdom of letting him homeschool for a semester. During those months, he was able to concentrate on adopting healthier habits. He made new friends, and by the time he went back to school, he was stronger and ready to deal. While I still don't advocate homeschooling as a long-term solution, if it's just for a semester or two to give someone time to regroup, I think it can be helpful. It certainly was for Zach.

If you need time to regroup too, talk to your parents about it. It doesn't necessarily have to mean temporary homeschooling. Sometimes, a small change can make a big difference. The secret is to find outlets, like Zach did with working out, that help you grow as a person and feel better about yourself. Ask your parents or an adult at school you like and trust to help you figure out what will work best for you. Go beyond your comfort zone. If you've never tried dance, sign up for a class. If you've been curious about yoga but nervous you wouldn't be good at it, go for it anyway. The more you push past the negative thoughts that hold you back, the stronger and more confident you'll become. Take time right now to think about an activity that you've never done before that would not only be a healthy addition to your routine, but that you'd enjoy. Then, get busy making it happen. Small steps are the start to big changes. If you'd like some ideas on where to start, shoot me an e-mail. I'm always here, ready to cheer you on!

One more thing before I go. Zach tried locking himself in his room and his parents eventually had to take the lock off the door to get in. This isn't a good thing to do. Not only can it be dangerous, but you can't lock the problem away. If you're feeling that desperate, it's time to talk to someone. Remember, I'm here.

# CHAPTER SIX

# Aamina

Hello. I'm Aamina. I'm sixteen and a sophomore. My story isn't just about school bullies; it's a whole town.

I'm Muslim American. For a long time, I was the only Muslim at school. It wasn't easy at first, but I worked hard at making friends and after a while, most of the kids accepted me. There were a couple of guys in my class who called anyone with olive skin a terrorist. I ignored them. I had a good group of friends and was busy with all kinds of stuff. I did drama club, volleyball, and I was on the yearbook committee too. Even though I was raised Muslim, I didn't act super religious. I had posters of my favorite celebs on my wall, like Harry Styles from One Direction. He's *so* fine, OMG.

My parents were constantly getting on my case for being on my cell phone too much. I got into mega trouble over the summer for wearing black eyeliner. My mom lets me wear "natural" makeup, like blush and sheer lip gloss, but I'm not allowed to wear eye makeup yet. Senior year, Mom says. My BFF Courtney and I were hanging out by her house, and we started playing with her older sister's makeup. Before I knew it, we had done these totally cool makeovers on each other. When her sister asked us if we wanted to go to the mall, we said sure, and forgot to wash our faces before we left. Oops! Guess who we bumped into in the food court! My mom! She was mad. Courtney's mom wasn't happy either. We both got punished. No cell phones for a week. I think that was way harsh.

My family lived in a nice suburb and everyone pretty much knew each other. My parents owned a couple of popular restaurants in town. Even though my mom worked a lot of hours, she never missed a PTA meeting, and was super active in the community. My dad was a total golf freak. When he wasn't at one of the restaurants, he'd be on the golf course.

A few of the neighbors acted a little uncomfortable around us sometimes, especially if there was some story about terrorism in the news, like after the bombing at the Boston Marathon, but it would usually blow over. That all changed when more Muslim families started moving into the neighborhood, and storefronts began going up with signs in Arabic. People we'd known for years, who had never seemed prejudiced, started acting differently around us. Everything got so weird. Some of my friends' parents stopped eating at my family's restaurants and when we'd ask why, they'd come up with lame excuses. My dad got squeezed out of his regular Sunday golf game. Every year, my mom was picked as chairman of the Chamber of Commerce annual fundraiser. Not anymore. They chose someone else.

It was happening at school too. I heard a bunch of kids talking about how their parents were complaining, "Terrorists are taking over the town." When a story ran on the front page of the newspaper that a mosque was being built on Main Street, a local lawyer, one of my dad's golf buddies, got a bunch of business owners together and sued the township to stop it. They lost, and within a month, a group of "concerned citizens" were picketing the construction site every day. Many of them were moms and dads in the school district.

A lot of my friends stopped hanging out with me. They said they weren't "allowed to" anymore. Courtney pulled away. That hurt because we had been besties since middle school. She went on vacations with me, and I spent two weeks every summer with her and her family at their lake house. We told each other everything. We did practically everything together.

I never felt more alone in my life.

Even kids at school who just looked foreign were screwed. This boy M.J., whose dad owns a gas station, stopped getting invited to parties. He told me his parents were thinking about moving because ever since the mosque thing, they were getting threatening phone calls. M.J. and his family aren't even Muslim. They're Hindu. My parents said we were living in "a town divided." Maybe it was always there but now it was out in the open.

M.J. got beaten up after school. The kids who did it got away with it too because M.J. was too afraid to tell on them. I got tormented daily on Facebook and Twitter. Some of the stuff that was posted made me sick. I went to the school counselor and the principal. They listened and then didn't do anything.

I tried to make friends with some of the new Muslim kids, but most of them were from strict religious families and had been raised in the Middle East. It was like we were from two different worlds.

I didn't fit in anywhere anymore and it sucked.

I hid what was happening at school from my parents because I didn't want to stress them out. The restaurants weren't doing well, and my mom was looking for a job to help with expenses. A year earlier, everything was fine. All this freaking out because of a mosque and a few grocery stores in strip malls . . . it was crazy.

There were editorials in the paper that the mosque was just a front for al-Qaeda. Then, and this was so crazy, it was like out of a TV episode, a mosque about fifteen miles away got busted in a huge FBI investigation. It was all over the news for weeks. It turns out it really *was* a front for a terrorist cell. A ton of people were arrested, and the news coverage showed them being hauled off in handcuffs by Homeland Security. It sucked because it just made things in my neighborhood worse. The number of protesters picketing the construction site tripled. I hated that there were actually people who believed if you were Muslim you were automatically a terrorist. That's like saying all Christians blow up abortion clinics or all Mexicans sell drugs.

That night, I heard my mom crying. I didn't know what to do. It was usually the other way around. I went up to her and hugged her and asked her what was wrong.

She said, "I went on your Facebook page tonight."

I told her everything. She handled it better than I thought she would. We both agreed that instead of trying to go back to the principal we would look for support outside of school. There had to be other Muslim Americans going through what we were, and we decided it was time to take action.

The next day, Mom and I went on the computer and Googled Muslim-American organizations. We found a Muslim Mother-Daughter Club. Their website read, "Mothers and Daughters Making a Difference." They had several chapters throughout the country. The nearest one was about a hundred miles away. On their website, it said they were hosting their annual Mother's Day dinner on Saturday, and tickets were still available. Mom and I immediately called and bought two. We decided to leave on Friday and make it an adventure. We stayed at this neat little bed and breakfast and talked and talked. It was good for both of us. The next day, we got manis and pedis and did fun girl stuff. The dinner was being held at an old country club. When we arrived, it was like something in a movie. The ballroom was decorated in beautiful spring colors, and every table had a nametag showing where to sit. When we checked in, everyone was so friendly. When we got to our table, we felt welcome right away. Some of the mothers and daughters were very traditional and wearing Muslim clothes with their heads covered. Others were like Mom and me and totally westernized. The one thing we all knew was that we were dealing with fear and prejudice that had become harder since 9/11.

Everybody shared their stories over dinner, and as I listened, I realized none of us was alone, that just because we felt that way sometimes didn't make it true. One of the girls at our table said she and her mom worked with her social studies teacher to start a religious tolerance campaign at her school. They included students from all types of backgrounds, Jewish, Buddhist, Catholic; even an atheist student gave a presentation. She said it had a pretty big impact and that it helped a lot of kids.

After the dinner, there was an awards ceremony. It was awesome. Later, we met the president of the club. We told her we lived too far to attend regular meetings. She suggested we start a chapter in our community. When Mom and I got back home, that's exactly what we did. We have about twenty members now, and we're growing. Everything we do is about creating tolerance and understanding. Do I still miss my old friends? Yeah, but at least now, I know I'm making a difference for other kids like me who have been bullied because of their culture or religion.

The mosque finally got built. It's beautiful. Some people are still pissed off about it, but everyone is freaking out way more about this big garbage company that wants to put a landfill outside of town. That's like a garbage dump where they bury toxic waste. It's gross. My parents are on a committee with a ton of other people raising money to fight it. They say that every once in a while, they'll get a hostile vibe from someone, but they've learned to deal.

Courtney and I are friends again. She and her parents felt bad about what happened. I've totally forgiven her. She was getting pressure from everyone. Dad's restaurants are doing a little better too. Mom and I are busier than ever with our Mother-Daughter Club. We're working with the school district to launch an anti-bullying campaign and we've already got a famous speaker coming to talk to all the students.

If you're getting messed with at school or in your community because you're from a different culture or religion, you don't have to face it alone. Check out clubs or organizations in your area where you can meet other people who share the same background. If your family belongs to a church, temple, mosque, synagogue, or other place of worship, see if it has a teen group. If not, start one. The more you reach out, the better things will get.

Before I go, there's something I want to say. When Jodee asked me to talk to you, I didn't want to. I was still too upset about what happened. She said it might make me feel better. She was right. I didn't realize until right now how strong I am. You're stronger than you think too. Hang in there, okay?

*Aamina, you and your family should be proud of yourselves for your strength, and your ability to forgive. Prejudice comes from fear and ignorance. People are scared of what they don't understand. It's not even personal most of the time, even though it sure can feel that way.*

*I think it's wonderful you and your mom reached out to the Mother-Daughter Club and started a chapter. Not only did it give you both comfort and support; it allowed you to make a difference in your own community. It's easy to feel alone and isolated, but if you take the time to look for a solution, one can almost always be found.*

*I'd like to take a moment to discuss hurt and anger. If you're going through something similar to Aamina, or any type of bullying or rejection, it can mess with your head for a while. Even if things get better, you may still feel angry. That's okay. Just because you get through it, it doesn't mean all those feelings disappear right away. It takes time to process emotions, and you have to be patient with yourself. A therapist can also be helpful. It's important if you do see a therapist though, that you feel comfortable with that person. Therapists are human too. When I was a teen, I went through a few before I met one I clicked with. It's a process. Don't be too hard on yourself.*

Lastly, when Aamina was being cyber-bullied, she was afraid to tell her parents because she didn't want to burden them. Her mom sensed something was wrong anyway. Not knowing what's going on with a child and wondering what could be wrong is a much bigger burden on a parent and way worse than just being told the truth. Don't hide stuff from your parents even if you think it's for a good reason like trying to protect them. If you're honest and upfront when something happens, it prevents your mom and dad from having to guess. When an adult is worried, their imagination can go all over the place. By the time they do find out the facts, everyone is freaking out. Be open and honest from the beginning.

As always, if you need an ear, I'm here.

# CHAPTER SEVEN

# Trinity

I'm Trinity. I'm a freshman. I'm pretty plain-looking I guess. I've got shoulder-length brown hair and brown eyes, and I don't wear a lot of makeup. It makes my acne worse. My mom started me on Proactiv, but I still get breakouts. I'm good at school and my grades are mostly As and Bs, except for a C+ in math, but that was because I missed a lot of school earlier this year. This is the first time I've talked about it to anyone. The reason I was absent so much was that I was super depressed. The doctor said she didn't think I had a "depressive disorder." She told my parents it was "situational," which basically means that my life sucked and I couldn't stand it anymore.

I felt invisible at school. Kids might say hi to me or ask me about some homework thing, but I wasn't on anyone's social radar. In Lit class, we learned about round characters and flat characters. Round characters are the main people in the story, the ones you care about what happens to them. They have lives and feelings, and you get to totally know them. Sometimes, you even miss them after you finish the book. Flat characters are minor and only in scenes where they're needed for the plot to work. No one notices them or remembers them. That's how I felt, like if someone wrote a novel about our school, I'd be one of the flat characters.

A lot of people assumed that because I wasn't in a clique, I was a loner. I hated being by myself. I would have given anything to have a group of friends to hang out with. I tried but it's like I was cursed or something, like with this girl Kaylee and her friends. My locker was in the same section as theirs. They would always wait until the last minute to go to class. I wanted to make friends with them, but I was too intimidated, so instead I'd hang around, pretending to be looking for something in my locker, hoping they'd talk to me. I looked up to Kaylee. She wasn't a bitch like a lot of the other popular girls at school. She was nice. Her BFF, Megan, was too. They always dressed so cool, and boys totally crushed on them. One day, Kaylee noticed me standing there alone before lunch period and invited me to sit at her table. On the way to the cafeteria, I was so nervous I kept running into the bathroom to make sure I looked okay. A teacher stopped me in the hall and asked if I needed to go to the nurse's office. I had to race across the building to make lunch before the bell rang. By the time I got to Kaylee and Megan's table, there wasn't any more room. Kaylee's boyfriend, Jamal, and two of his buddies had decided to hog the last three seats. They always ate at the jock table. Why couldn't they have picked another day to sit there? Every day for a week, I passed by Kaylee's table at lunchtime, hoping for an empty seat, but Jamal and those guys were always there, and the school was really strict about how many people were allowed per table. After a while, Kaylee forgot all about inviting me. I know she was just being nice. But if I just could have had that chance . . .

I wasn't bullied. I was left out. In a lot of ways, it was harder. If someone hits you or does horrible, mean things to you, you can tell yourself, there's something wrong with that person. But if you're ignored all the time, treated like you don't even exist, it makes you think there must be something wrong with *you*.

When Kaylee asked me to sit at her table, I was so happy. I wanted to hang out with her and her friends so much. Sometimes on Monday mornings, I'd hear them talking about what they did on the weekend, and I'd close my eyes and imagine I was a part of their world, the parties and sleepovers, the cool trips to the mall where everyone would meet at Starbucks and then all go to someone's house after to chill, the awesome secrets they shared about who was going out with who and who thought who was hot, and who flirted with who and how far they went, oh my gosh, so amazing. I'd have given anything to know what that felt like, to never have to worry about whether you'd have something to do on Saturday night, to not have to worry when you were late for an assembly if anyone had saved you a spot, to go to home games with "the gang" and get tons of texts from people wanting to know what you were doing after. Most kids like Kaylee and her friends took that stuff for granted. It was normal to them. But for kids like me, those things were like the privileges of royalty or something.

Part of the reason I felt so depressed was that I'd totally built up high school in my head. I hated the drama in middle school. Everyone told me things would get better in high school. I spent the whole summer after eighth grade seeing every movie I could about high school. I saw *Mean Girls, Superbad, American Pie, Juno, Napoleon Dynamite*, plus a ton of others, but my favorite was this really old movie, like totally ancient, but *so awesome*, called *Grease*, with John Travolta and Olivia Newton-John.

In the movie, Olivia Newton-John is this new student from Australia, and she's like this total goody two-shoes who falls in love with John Travolta, except it happens over the summer, and when they get back to school, he pretends not to be into her anymore because he thinks it will make him look uncool to his friends to be all mushy over one girl. The whole movie is about Sandy, that's Olivia Newton-John's character, finally fitting in and getting Danny back, that's Travolta's character. Sandy goes from nerd to stone-cold hottie in this movie, and I fantasized about doing it too, like going from being me to Kaylee.

It was the best movie ever. It gave me hope. But by second quarter of this year, I realized it was all just BS, that real life sucked, and that I'd probably always be invisible. I wasn't comfortable putting myself out there like a lot of the other kids. I didn't like wearing tight shirts to show off my chest and stuff; it made me feel weird and self-conscious. Plus, I felt fat in super-tight clothes. In high school, you have to "bring it." I bought an outfit at Forever 21 once but I never had the guts to wear it.

My parents knew something was wrong when I started to get so tired I couldn't go to school. That's when I missed all those days that screwed up my math grade. My doctor checked me for everything: mono, chronic fatigue syndrome, thyroid issues, anemia. The tests always came back negative, so my parents finally made me see a therapist. Thank God all I had to do was talk to her once a week and not take any psych meds. It helped to get stuff off my chest, and anything was better than meds. Some kids at school were on them and it made them more miserable.

Okay, so fast-forward to right after Christmas break. It was anti-bullying week at our school. I was in the gym at an assembly. The whole school was there. Jodee was the speaker. That's how we met. I'll tell you that part in a minute. She had just finished her presentation. She relived scenes from when she was bullied at school and then talked about how it made her feel. She told us that it still messes with her head even though she's an adult. It was intense. The kids who got bullied a lot were crying. This one girl was so upset, Jodee had to go over and comfort her. It was Shondra. She carried her books in an "I Heart Justin Bieber" bag, and she brought her lunch in a Justin Bieber lunchbox. I *love* the Biebs, I think he's hot too, but you just don't *do* stuff like that in high school. Everyone made fun of her. Shondra was always asking if I wanted to go to the mall or Starbucks after school, but I was afraid if I hung out with her, I'd get made fun of too, so I'd make up an excuse or take the long way to my locker to avoid her. After a while, she stopped asking. Sometimes, after school, I'd see her standing all by herself outside waiting for her mom to pick her up. She'd notice me and smile and wave, and I wanted to wave back, to be friends with her, but instead, I pretended I didn't see.

I felt sick.

Jodee was asking the audience if there were any questions. I raised my hand. She came over and handed me the microphone. I was scared but I knew I had to do it.

"I'm a bully."

Some kids laughed; others looked uncomfortable. I kept going.

"There's someone I was really mean to and I want to make it up to them," I said. Then, I took a deep breath, stood up, and walked over to where Shondra was sitting. I told her how sorry I was and asked if she'd still want to be friends with me. By now, the gym was silent. Everyone was waiting to see what would happen. Shondra didn't say anything; she just nodded her head and then got up and hugged me. A couple of the other kids who had been crying came over and group hugged us. People started clapping and cheering. After the assembly, Jodee asked to meet with Shondra and me. She told us how proud she was of both of us.

That was a few months ago. Since then, Shondra and I have been pretty tight. She still gets bullied, but it's a little better than it was, and kids stick up for her now. I don't feel as invisible as I did before, and I try to do one brave thing every day. Like yesterday, Jamal and his friends weren't at lunch, so I asked Kaylee and Megan if I could sit with them. They were like, absolutely, and we spent the whole period together, and I wasn't even nervous.

*Trinity, thanks for the props about my talk. I'm glad it made an impact. Some of your classmates may revert to old habits, but those who really want to change how they feel about themselves and others will keep trying. That's what's important. I am so, so proud of you and Shondra. I'd like to give you both*

an assignment and I'd like you to share it with Kaylee and Megan and their friends and ask them to do it too.

There are two types of bullied kids in a school—the "overtly bullied," who get teased and messed with in obvious ways like Shondra was, and the "invisible student," who may not be bullied in the traditional sense or even intentionally excluded but who isn't on anyone's social radar either. That's who you were, Trinity. Some can be both at different times.

Here's your assignment. I want you to pay closer attention to the kids at your school who are having a hard time fitting in, and I want you to reach out to one of those kids and make him feel included. It could be as simple as an invitation to sit with you at lunch or to hang and study together during free period. The whole point is to make that person feel wanted. The overtly bullied students will probably be easier to spot because you see them getting bullied. The invisible students will likely be harder to identify. The best way to do that is to close your eyes and imagine someone has just invited you to a party and said, "It'll be so cool. Everyone will be there!" Certain faces will automatically pop into your head when you hear the word "everyone." Which faces don't you see? They could be invisible students.

If you're listening and are saying to yourself, "I'm one of those invisible kids," I know how lonely and frustrating it can be. Trinity got so depressed that for weeks, she didn't have the energy to go to school. The ironic part is that without even being aware of it at the time, she was making Shondra feel exactly how she felt. Trinity made huge progress and so can you.

First, and you've been hearing me say this since you got here, find an adult you trust and ask for support. Whether it's one of your parents, the parent of a friend, your school counselor, *or a teacher you feel comfortable opening up to, don't suffer in silence. Second, I understand wanting to be liked by the popular kids, but don't let it make you less open to being friends with other people. There are two kinds of popular kids at a school. The elite leader is the nice member of the cool crowd who doesn't like to exclude anyone and cares about other people's feelings. The elite tormentor is the mean popular kid who creates a lot of nasty drama and will turn on you if you hang out with anyone she doesn't like. Elite tormentors are never true friends to begin with. Don't let them have power over you. Elite leaders, like Kaylee and Megan, will not only respect you for being friends with all different types of students; they'll admire you.*

## CHAPTER EIGHT

# Joshua

I want you to read this. It's from my journal. After you read it, I'll tell you what happened. I'm Joshua, by the way. Sorry, I always forget to introduce myself. I'm seventeen and a senior in high school.

Journal Entry, October 14

I'm a mistake. I shouldn't have been born. Everyone has at least one giant f___up. I was God's. I wish my dad had been too drunk to do my mom the night she got pregnant. I never asked to be born. Why can't you get to see what your life will be like before you're born, like on a big video screen or something, and if you don't think you can handle it, you're allowed to bail? Maybe that's what miscarriages are. I read once that the soul doesn't enter the body until you're born. So maybe the souls of babies that never got born changed their minds about coming down here at the last minute. They're probably all hanging out, chilling, putting off having to be on earth. I bet there's like this rule that you only get so many video previews of different lives, but after a certain amount, you have to pick one, and if you don't, you're stuck with the last video you were shown. Maybe that's what happened to me. I hate it here. It's like being in jail for something I didn't do.

Dad was drunk again tonight. What else is f___ing new? At least he didn't puke all over himself this time. Last weekend he got so wasted, he didn't even make it to the bathroom. He threw up in the hall and I had to wipe it all up; it was nasty. Mom is useless as usual. When I left for school this morning, she was already gulping down pills. She always goes through all the anti-depressants and anxiety meds way too fast, like she runs out before she should. They make her like a vegetable. The woman can't handle sh_t. It's like living with one of those zombies from *The Walking Dead*.

I've been looking on the Internet for ways to commit suicide. Most of them are gross. But there are a couple that are really cool. Sh_t, I gotta bounce. Tuli's screaming again.

Yeah, my family is totally messed up. I didn't always hate my dad. I know I can be harsh in my journal sometimes, but I get pissed off. My dad always was a partier. He and my mom met at an Ozzy concert in the eighties. Mom has depression. After I was born, it got worse, my dad says. She was moody all the time and he hated coming home. I don't remember this but my dad says my mom had to be put in the hospital a couple of times to get her meds straight. Her doctor's a total f___up. It's like Mom's always in a trance.

Anyway, we were talking about my dad. Sorry, I get so ADHD. Dad did stuff with me when I was little and all the kids in the neighborhood thought he was cool because he was into Zeppelin and AC/DC, and all those awesome rock bands, and his hair was long, and he dressed cool and sh_t, not like a lot of the other dads who were *such* geeks.

Everything got harder when my mom had my sister, Tuli. Don't get me wrong. I love my sister but she's special-needs. She's got Down's, and she's like a three-year-old even though she's really twelve. She's really sweet but sometimes she throws a fit. If Mom is having one of her "bad days" she can't handle it. Dad's good with Tuli if he's around, and he's sober, which is like hardly ever because when he is home, the first thing he does is grab a beer, and then keeps 'em coming. I take care of Tuli. She goes to a special school during the day. I watch out for her at night. Mom tries, but she just can't deal. Like when Tuli was screaming, it was because there was a spider in the bathroom. Mom just stood there freaking out watching it crawl across the sink. I wanted to shake her and say, can't you just be a mother for once in your stupid life! I got a Dixie cup and took my toothbrush and kind of nudged the spider into the cup, and then I took it outside.

Ever since I read *Charlotte's Web* in grade school, I don't kill spiders. No f___ing way. Tuli was still so scared, Mom and I had to sit and watch TV with her until she got sleepy.

I know Mom wanted to be better, and some days she almost seemed normal, but then the next day, she'd get so dark and sad that anything could set her off. I tried to stay away from her when she was like that, but Tuli didn't know any better. Sometimes Mom would rip into her over nothing. I hated Mom when she lost it around Tuli.

I wanted to try out for basketball but I was too afraid to leave Tuli alone. I talked to my school counselor, and she wanted to report my parents to social services. I never went to her again. And I couldn't ask any relatives for help. My grandparents were in Florida living in some complex for old people, and my mom's sister had four kids. Anyways, living at home didn't totally suck. I could be on the Internet as long as I wanted, and I didn't have a curfew.

Most kids would have killed not to have their parents in their face all the time. Between you and me, I wish mine were in my face more. Not that I wanted a bunch of rules or anything, but sometimes I felt like if I disappeared my parents wouldn't even notice.

Here's the thing though. I'm going to be a writer when I get out of here. All the sh_t I've had to deal with is golden. It'll make me a killer writer. People who never have anything bad happen to them can't be writers. Name one great book or amazing song written by someone who's happy? Pain keeps it real. Yeah, I've thought about offing myself, but I bet a lot of famous writers have too. That's what keeps me going, writing. And Tuli.

I'm supposed to be talking to you about the thing at school. Okay, so, like everybody at my school is in a clique. If you're not, nobody pays attention to you. Some kids just have a couple of friends, they're like the clique rejects, and they get looked down on. I try to be nice to everyone, but it's not like it matters. I get trash-talked anyway. I know how the other kids see me. They think I'm some psycho loner. To them, I'm just this dude with a beat-up old black notebook who doesn't do any sports or anything and who hardly ever talks to anyone.

I don't mean to be all closed up on purpose. It's like my head is this giant hose and ideas keep gushing out of it, and feelings and thoughts, and I have to write them down. When I write, I can get so intense that I don't know how much time has gone by. Like once, I missed the whole first half of English because I was pissed off about something and so lost in my journal, I didn't hear the bell ring. My journal isn't something I do; it's a place where I go when this place hurts too much.

A lot of kids at school gossip about me and say twisted sh_t. I even heard there was a rumor once that I hacked my parents with an ax and had my sister locked in a room. Someone told the principal, and a cop came by the house for a "wellness" check. Thank God we were all home that night and Dad wasn't looped. The crazy-assed sh__head who started the rumor finally admitted he did it on a dare. And get this, a couple of weeks before that happened, someone at school tweeted I was a foster kid and my parents were drug addicts.

Sometimes I fantasized about revenge, and I'd write these sick poems, about how one day, I'd be a famous writer, and the mean kids at school would end up nowhere in life with nothing, and while I was getting awards for my writing and my books were on bestseller lists all over the world, and I got rich and famous, they'd be stuck with sh__ty careers in sh__ty marriages with kids who hated them, and they'd eat junk food and get fat, and not have any true friends, and be miserable. I'd feel way better after.

I had one friend at school, this girl Skate. That was her nickname because she was so into skateboarding. We had a ton in common. We were both clique rejects, seriously into alternative bands like Muse, Imagine Dragons, Arctic Monkeys, Linkin Park. We thought they were cool *way* before anyone else did. We'd listen for hours and read to each other from our journals. As long as I had Skate and my journal, I could deal. Then, Skate moved. Her dad got a big job in New York. School already sucked but without Skate, it sucked worse. Now I didn't have anyone to sit with anymore at lunch or hang out with, or tell my secrets to. Skate's parents were hip to my situation. I never said much and they were cool, they didn't pry, but they always let me know they were there for me. Without them, my life had this huge hole in it.

About a week after Skate moved, I was on my way to class and I noticed everyone looking at me weird, laughing and whispering. Then, they started yelling sh_t . . .

"Too bad you *weren't* a miscarriage, psycho!"

"Hey, want some help Googling cool ways to off yourself, freakazoid?"

The second I heard those words I *knew.*

"Hey, asshole, can I do your zombie mommy?"

I put my iPod on and cranked it as loud as it would go to drown out the screaming in my head. The school D.A.R.E. officer came up to me and asked me to follow him to the principal's office. I could feel the gossip as we went down the hall. It was the longest walk of my life.

When we got there, the principal handed me my journal. He said the janitor found it stuffed at the bottom of a garbage can in the cafeteria. Someone had stolen it from my locker, copied a bunch of pages, and posted them anonymously on Tumblr. The school did an investigation but never found out who was responsible.

Sometimes what you think is the worst thing that could ever happen to you ends up being the best thing. I found out the school principal went through a lot when he was in high school too. He told me he'd help me but I had to work with him and do what he asked. If you're having a hard time like me, don't assume the school can't help. Some principals are dicks for sure, but some are cool and really care, like mine. If your principal wants to help you deal, don't automatically blow him off. Try trusting him. It really does work sometimes.

Sorry, back to what I was saying. I had to talk to the district social worker at least twice a week and if I had any more suicidal thoughts I had to tell her right away and never hide stuff like that again. My principal also told me to give him the names of the kids at school who had said those horrible things to me after my journal pages got posted. He said if someone is that mean, they could be in trouble and need help. If you're ever in the same spot, and you're afraid it'll make things worse if you tell, do it anyway.

I did. It turned out one of them was taking steroids for wrestling and his head wasn't right because of it. His parents actually told the principal to thank me for saying something. They said they would never have known if I hadn't, and this kid's doctor said he could have died.

The hardest part of this whole thing was dealing with my parents. The principal agreed with my counselor about social services, that my parents needed a serious wake-up call. So I spilled, told the truth about everything, Dad's drinking, Mom's depression, her yelling at Tuli all the time. I felt sick watching the social worker take notes, like I was betraying my parents, but I knew it was the right thing.

That was six months ago. Dad is in AA now. It's one of the conditions of Tuli and me being able to stay at home. Mom has a new doctor, and he changed her meds and put her in a support group for people with depression. There's one for their family members too, which Dad and I go to. It's pretty cool and I even met this girl there. We've been hanging out and she wants to be a writer too. Skate and I Skype constantly, and my dad's letting me visit her this summer. She said she'd take me to Rockefeller Center and we could walk over to Simon & Schuster, this big publishing house, and check it out. Maybe one day they'll publish my first book.

*Joshua, I'm so sorry you had to go through so much and that you felt alone for so long. What your classmates did to you was unspeakable. A journal is a sacred part of oneself and for it to be violated is terrifying and painful. Please promise me you'll honor your agreement with your principal, and if you ever have suicidal thoughts again, you'll tell your social worker, and you won't keep it inside.*

*For anyone else who's listening, suicide is NEVER the answer. If you EVER feel yourself going there, turn to an adult you trust and get support. RIGHT NOW. Life is full of wonder and surprises. Your life is precious and meaningful. You ARE loved.*

*Joshua, let's get back to you for a moment. I want you to know you absolutely did the right thing, finally letting your principal and the social worker step in at home. I know how hard it was to tell the truth about your parents' struggles, but sometimes, you have to tell on an adult for the same reason you would another kid—to help them. If someone is bullying another person and you allow it to continue, that's called being a bystander. If someone is hurting themselves, like by drinking too much or abusing prescription meds, and you don't do anything, that's called being an enabler.*

*Think about all the people you helped by being honest. You may have saved the life of your classmate who was doing steroids. Your dad was slipping deeper into alcoholism, and now he's committed to recovery. Your mom was lost and now she's got support and is finding her way back. You're a hero, Joshua.*

## CHAPTER NINE

# Tiffany

I don't even know where to start. It was like watching a horror movie except it was my own life. When I look back now, it's hard for me to breathe. I should be dead. I wanted to be dead. Yeah, I screwed up. But no one deserves what they did to me. *No one.*

I'm Tiffany. My friends call me Tiff, or at least they did before I lost them. I graduated high school this summer. Let me tell you what happened senior year. Before you even ask, yes, all of it's true. Every word.

Freshman year I started dating Matthew. Every chick at school was into Matthew. OMG, he was beyond. He was on the football team, got killer grades, and had the biggest personality at school. He looked like Ryan Gosling but way cuter. I was like totally in love with him since seventh grade. He was nice to me in middle school but he wasn't crushing on me or anything. After high school started, I kind of blossomed. I went from no boobs to killer ones. Even I liked looking at them, LOL. My body changed in other ways too. I got thinner and my skin cleared up. Guys actually started checking me out. It was beyond, like a total rush. When my BFF, Paisley, said Matthew was into me, I was off the charts happy. Our first date, we walked over to Marcus Theatres, and saw *Jackass 3*. LMAO. I never thought laughing with another person could be romantic but it *so* is!

After the movie, we hung out at his house. His parents were at some business thing and we had the whole place to ourselves. We started making out. It was intense. I'd only ever had two dates in my life, and the first one didn't count because it was my dad's lawyer's kid, who was a geek. Matthew and I were both getting all out of breath, the kissing was beyond, and he started to touch me down there. I got all nervous. I was still a virgin.

He asked me what's wrong. I told him I can't yet.

I was so scared he'd be mad, but he wasn't. He joked about having to take a cold shower, and then he put his hand on my cheek and said it was okay, that I was worth waiting for. From that night on, Matthew and I were totally a couple. Not only were Matthew and I madly over the top for each other, but his best friend Luke and my BFF Paisley were into each other too. The four of us did everything together. We hung out after school and on weekends. We had these awesome parties. Everybody came. I was never popular before.

It was so weird being a part of that crowd. I knew a lot of people only wanted to be my friend because I was with Matthew. It's like this term we learned in economics, "proxy." It's kind of hard to explain but it's like if your BFF got grounded and you felt bad she couldn't go out, so you hung with her at home and stayed in too, you could say you got grounded by proxy. I was popular by proxy. I know it should have bugged me. A little voice in my head kept saying over and over, "These people aren't your true friends." But I was too busy partying and having fun to care. I had everything I wanted, a hot boyfriend, a killer social life. My parents loved Matthew and his parents loved me. When I was ready to go all the way with him, my mom was so cool about it. She took me to the gynecologist and got me a prescription for the pill. I loved high school. I didn't think anything could go wrong. I should have listened to that little voice.

Junior year, I began applying to colleges. I wanted to major in political science and I was nervous about getting into a good school. My first choice was Georgetown or American University in DC. Matthew didn't want me to go out of state. He'd always been kind of possessive, like he'd get super pissed off when I'd hang out with my favorite cousin because she had a lot of cute guy friends. I figured it was because he loved me so much, so I just put up with it, but after a while he really started freaking me out. He wanted to know where I was going and what I was doing all the time. The more college applications I sent in, the worse he got.

Then, we had this huge fight right before summer break. I was sick of him trying to control me. I finally lost it. We said stuff I can't even repeat here. It was bad. I was sick to my stomach for days. I texted him a ton of times but he wouldn't text me back. I tried calling, but it went to voicemail. I'd leave him a message, listen to it, and then erase it and start all over again. I was a mess. My parents were worried, so when my aunt and uncle invited me for the summer to their beach house to hang with my cousin, my parents were like, *"You're going."*

My cousin's friends were way cool. They were into kite-boarding and kale smoothies. OMG, the whole kale thing grossed me out at first but then I started to like them too! Anyway, this one guy, Cory, was hot. He was going into his sophomore year at BU. We totally clicked. He even taught me how to kiteboard! Cory and I kissed a few times. He was a really, really good kisser. One night, me and Cory were hanging out at the beach. It was a big group of us. We had this awesome bonfire going and music playing, and Matthew's and my song came on, Emeli Sandé's and Labrinth's "Beneath Your Beautiful." We used to make out to it all the time. Hearing it made me miss him. I tried to call him but it went to his voicemail, so I left a message. All night I kept checking my cell phone to see if he'd called or texted but there was nothing. I was beyond upset. I had a beer, and then some Jell-O shots, and then another beer. Cory was drinking too. One of the parents had gotten us a kegger for the party.

I don't know who brought the Jell-O shots. They went down really easy. I got drunk. Cory came up to me and kissed me. All these feelings were swirling in my head. Cory took me to the boat dock, and we did it under the awning. All I kept thinking about was Matthew. Afterward, I felt queasy. Cory asked me what was wrong. I bent over the dock and threw up.

Fast-forward to September. Long story short, Matthew found out about Cory. I hate Facebook. Matthew freaked. Luke and Paisley freaked. Everybody in our group took Matthew's side. I tried to explain my side of the story but no one would listen. Matthew was the most popular guy at school. No one wanted to risk being on the outs with him. He was the victim, and I was the selfish bitch who cheated on him. Everyone turned on me. People wrote "slut" across my locker.

Someone stuck a *used* condom in my backpack with a note, "F___ you, bitch." At lunch, I'd go to the school library to hide. I couldn't eat anyway. Nothing mattered. The bullying I got online was worse. Facebook, Tumblr, Foursquare, you name it, I was being trash-talked on some website. It was constant. At first, I responded, but that only made them post more mean things. Then, when I tried ignoring it, I started to get threatening text messages. My parents didn't know what to do. They went to the school, the police, and no one could do anything. When the acceptance letter from Georgetown came in, I wasn't even excited.

This went on for almost three months. Then, the weekend before Thanksgiving, Paisley called and said she wasn't mad at me anymore, that everybody really missed me, and even Matthew had forgiven me. She said Luke's parents were out of town and that he was having a party that Friday night. "Please, please, *please* come," she said. "Everyone's going to be there."

My parents begged me not to go.

The night of the party, Luke and Paisley answered the door. Something didn't feel right. There was no music on or any food out. They took me down to the basement. Everyone was just standing there, like they were waiting for me. There were three girls and four guys all from our group. I'd known them since seventh grade. Two of the boys grabbed me and held me down. The rest of them started beating me. They kicked me in the ribs, and they spat at me, and they punched me over and over. I saw blood all over my shirt and I tasted it in my mouth. I was crying. I pleaded with them to stop; they laughed, and hit me harder. "That's what you get for being a slut," one of them said. Then, they went upstairs and left me there. I tried to stand up, but I was too dizzy. I crawled out the back door and called my mom to pick me up. I spent the night in the ER.

The next day, a video of the beating went viral on YouTube. By Monday morning, tons of TV people were camping out at my house, the state's attorney's office said they were filing criminal charges against the kids in the video, and the superintendent of my school had already hired a lawyer to protect the district's ass.

Senior year was a black hole. My parents brought in a tutor to homeschool me the rest of the year. Matthew called a few times but because of the case I couldn't talk to him. After it went to trial, I found out he never knew anything. The case was constantly on TV and in the papers. The day I had to testify, I was scared to death, but I did it. I was proud of myself. Luke and Paisley and the kids who attacked me apologized in court to my family and me. The judge sentenced all of them to community service. A lot of people thought it was way too lenient a sentence and that they should have gotten a much worse punishment, but I was glad it was over. Besides, beating me up and videotaping it—they'll have to live with what they did forever. I was okay with that.

As I'm talking to you, I'm in my room packing the last of my stuff. I leave for Georgetown tomorrow. I'm so excited. My dorm is awesome and I've already met my new roommate. She wants to major in journalism. I can already tell we're going to be besties. I met my academic advisor too. I told her what I went through. She said that political science is the perfect major for me, that maybe one day I'll be able to use my experience to help others. YouTube shouldn't have let a video of someone getting beaten up be posted on their site, but they do what they want because they can. When I get out of college, I'm going to become a lobbyist and push for better laws. I can't wait to make my mark. Maybe if I hadn't gone through what I did, I wouldn't be as strong and determined. I definitely grew up.

If you're going through something bad, stay strong, too. There are going to be moments when you want to give up, when you don't have any faith in anyone or anything and you feel like you're dying one piece at a time. Scoop up the pieces and hold them together. Don't let yourself fall apart. You're braver than you think. You're not alone. You have all of us now and we believe in you.

*Tiff, your story affects me deeply. You suffered in every way that a person can, physically, emotionally, psychologically, and spiritually. You described your senior year as a "black hole." I know what that feels like. A friend of mine calls it being "in the jaws of the black dog." Some people let it take them down, while others like you, Tiff, come out swinging, more ready than ever to show the world what they're made of. We can all learn a lot from you.*

*There are just a couple of things I want to mention above and beyond the beating and the videotape. They may seem small by comparison, but they're not. First, let's talk about Matthew's possessiveness. When someone is possessive or jealous, it's a form of bullying. College is a fresh start for you, Tiff. Don't let any guy try to control you or hold you back from your dreams. Matthew should have been excited you were applying to Georgetown, not hoping to talk you out of it. Even though you didn't start really noticing his possessiveness until junior year, I suspect there were signs of it much earlier in the relationship. Next time, pay attention to the signs. That goes for everyone here, boys too. If you're into someone, and he doesn't support your independence, let him go. NO ONE has the right to control you, and more importantly, he shouldn't want to.*

*I also want to mention—and I wouldn't be a friend if I didn't—the kegger at the beach party. If any of you have ever been mad at your parents because you were having a party and they wouldn't let you have alcohol, please, cut them some slack. They did the right thing. Drinking also makes you more vulnerable to having sex when you may not be ready yet. It's easier to give in to pressure when you're buzzed or drunk. It's also how a lot of date rapes happen. If your parents are firm about not providing alcohol and you're jealous of the kids whose parents do, you've got things in reverse. Your parents are right. I promise.*

*If there are any parents listening in, DO NOT provide liquor for your kids' parties, unless they're adults over twenty-one. I know some of you want your kids to think you're cool, but breaking the law and putting them in danger isn't the way to do it.*

*You want to be cool? Listen to them without interrupting. Only give advice if they ask you for it. Don't ever say, "We'll see." You can do better than that. Don't protect them from reality. Prepare them for it. Last, be there for them even when it's hard.*

## CHAPTER TEN

# Autumn

Hi! I'm Autumn. I'm twelve. I'm a "little person." In the olden days, some people called us midgets. That's a bad, mean word. Dwarf is the nice word. I'm three feet eight inches tall, and even when I'm grown-up I won't be much more than four feet, the doctor says. I have curly blonde hair, my favorite color is blue, and my favorite movie ever, 'cause I love Amy Adams, is *Enchanted*. My favorite food is Reese's Peanut Butter Cups and I love grilled cheese sandwiches. Sometimes, when I have sleepovers, my mom makes peanut butter cup cookies. They're *so* good.

I have lots of friends at school. My best friend is Parker. She's really nice. She's got dark hair and looks like Selena Gomez except she can't sing, LOL. She likes to draw and says she's going to be an artist. I'm not good at drawing. I like doing puzzles and math. But what I like most is hanging out with all my friends. There's Parker, and Sandra, and Callie, and the boys in our clique are Cade, Cyrus, and Anthony. Sometimes Cody hangs out with us too but he's into soccer and always has tons of out-of-state games.

You'd really like my friends. This summer, we built a tree-house, and they made a special step for me so I could reach it. When all us kids showed the treehouse to our parents, my mom started to cry and hugged Parker. It still bothers her what happened with the kids at my last school. I'm over it kind of, but Mom worries. I wish she wouldn't. Everything is so way different now.

It happened last year in fifth grade. My dad got a new job. He's an accountant, and we had to move. I liked my old school. I went there since I was four years old, but it was too far away. I hated the new one. A lot of the kids were mean. No one talked to me or would hang out with me. This one girl Sophie wanted to be friends with me. We sat together at lunch a few times, but then she said she couldn't anymore because everyone was making fun of her for being nice to the "freak."

Recess was the worst. I'd watch everyone playing four-square and tag. They never let me play. A lot of times at recess, I'd pretend I didn't feel good, and I'd go to the nurse's and she'd do puzzles with me. This one kid, Bryce, was *so* mean. He told me the only thing I'd ever be good for was bowling. I was like, huh? Then someone e-mailed my parents a video he put on YouTube. Mom didn't want me to see it, but Dad said I had to so we could talk about it.

My parents had fights sometimes about that kind of stuff. Mom was super protective of me, like over the top, and Dad was into "preparing me for reality." I usually liked Dad's way better 'cause I got to do more things, but not this time. I wish I'd never seen that video. It showed a bunch of drunk people at some bowling alley and this big guy was throwing a little person down one of the lanes, except it looked all wet like a Slip 'N Slide. The little person was wearing a special suit and a helmet, and when he crashed into a bunch of pins and knocked them down, people clapped and cheered. It was bowling, but with a *human being*. You could hear all this laughing and everyone making fun of him, but he still kept doing it over and over. I felt bad for him. Under the video, Bryce wrote, "Look, it's Autumn!"

After we watched it, my parents showed me some articles on the Internet. They said it was called Midget Bowling, and that the people who do it are ignorant, and always will be, and that I should pray for them. I prayed all night. The next day Mom let me stay home from school and she went to talk to the principal. Bryce got suspended for a week, and his parents grounded him. They made him call and say he was sorry. Bryce was popular. All the kids at school said it was my fault he got into trouble. When he came back to class, they hated me more. I cried every day. I was glad when fifth grade was over.

All summer, all Mom talked about was homeschooling. I didn't want to. I knew I'd always be different, but just because you're different shouldn't mean you can't feel normal. Mom and Dad said okay, no homeschool, but on one condition: I'd go to a Catholic school. Most of the kids from fifth grade would be at the public middle school. Mom wanted me away from them.

I liked my new principal, Mrs. Baylor. Mom and I met her at the end of the summer. She wasn't a nun. She was a mom, too. I liked her because she didn't talk to me like I was a little girl. A lot of people do that. They treat me way younger than my age 'cause of my short stature. Oh yeah, that's the other thing you can say if you have dwarfism, that you're of "short stature." I like "little person" better because it has the word "person" in it.

Mrs. Baylor asked me lots of questions. The ones about fifth grade were hard. Mom looked sad. I said, "It's okay, Mom, I can do it." After I answered all Mrs. Baylor's questions, her secretary, Mrs. Fisk, took me on a tour of the school, while the grownups talked. I liked the school. It had a real theater where kids could put on plays. The library had every Nancy Drew book. I love Nancy Drew. My grandma read them when she was a kid, and so did my mom. I read one of Grandma's old ones once. It was *so* weird, like, Nancy didn't have a cell phone, and there was no Internet, and she used words like, "keen," OMG, *so* bizarre. I like the new ones way better. After we left the library, Mrs. Fisk showed me the cafeteria. It had big windows that looked out into a really cool garden with statues of saints. My favorite was Saint Francis. He protects all the animals.

The best part of my new school was the activity room. It had puzzles, the really hard kind, that even grownups take forever to finish. My new school had a math club too.

When I got back to Mrs. Baylor's office, I told her and Mom I was psyched. Mom smiled and said they wanted to talk to me about something. Mrs. Baylor said being the new student is never easy, especially if you're starting at a school where the other kids have known each other since kindergarten. She also said that when a person is different, kids can be mean, not because they don't like you, but because they're afraid.

"Some people, no matter what their age, are only comfortable with what they understand and are afraid of anything they don't," she said. "But sometimes if you help them understand they won't feel scared anymore."

That's what Mom and Mrs. Baylor wanted me to do when school started. Mom said it made sense, and that Mrs. Baylor was right, that I was too old now to just tell kids I was "born special" if they asked me what was wrong with me. Besides, I didn't want the kids at school to think there was something *wrong* with me. I wanted them to see the silly, super funny, really good at math, quicker than anyone at puzzles, best *ever* at hide-and-seek, totally into *Glee* person *inside* the little person.

This is what we did and this is what happened.

Mrs. Baylor sent a letter to all the parents about me. It talked about me being a little person, and that the first week of school, Mom and I were doing a special presentation on my condition, and kids could ask questions after. Mom and I spent the whole summer getting ready. The big day, we were nervous, but we were excited too. Dad helped us put everything in the car. We had big photos and pictures and tons of other cool stuff. When we got to school, Mrs. Baylor took us to the theater. All the kids were already in their seats. She introduced us. Mom and I gave our presentation.

We described the different types of dwarfism. We showed the photos we had, pictures of kids and grownups, and we explained the kind of dwarfism that I have, which is called achondroplasia. It's genetic. Genetic means it's already inside you before you're born. We even had this neat drawing of a human gene. We talked about why people with achondroplasia look different, like why our arms and legs are rounder and shorter than other people's.

Mom and I told funny stories from when I was growing up, like, this one time, when I was six. It was April Fools'

Day. I wanted to play a joke on my mom so I hid in the kitchen pantry under a box. Mom was looking all over for me. I heard her calling my name. I could tell she was freaking out. When she walked in the kitchen, I jumped out and yelled, "April Fool's!" She looked mad. Then, she took my squirt gun out of the junk drawer and started chasing me all over the kitchen. We were laughing so hard, Mom started peeing in her pants and had to run to the bathroom. It was the best April Fools' Day ever. It was *so* fun!

Mom told the kids, "Yeah, fun for *Autumn!*" Everybody laughed.

When we were done with the presentation, Mrs. Baylor asked if anyone had any questions. A girl raised her hand. Her question made me giggle. She asked if it was hard for me to reach the toilet. I showed her a picture of my stepping stool, and then let everyone pass it around. A boy raised his hand. He asked how I got stuff out of the fridge that was high up. I explained that sometimes I used the stool, but mostly, my mom put the food I always ate, like my after-school snacks, on the lower shelf. "Oh, cool," he said. By now, everybody was raising their hands. Some kids wanted to know if there was certain stuff I couldn't eat. I said that I'm allergic to strawberries, but not 'cause of my achondroplasia. I just had allergies.

Some girl shouted that she was allergic too. Then everyone started talking about their allergies. Mrs. Baylor and Mom were both smiling. Mrs. Baylor told everyone to quiet down and asked them to thank me and Mom for talking to them. Everybody cheered and clapped. Later that day, I got invited to two sleepovers and a birthday party. That's how Parker and I became BFFs and how I met all my friends. It was her birthday party. No strawberries though! She's allergic too.

I know the world is way bigger than just school and my friends. Dad says I'll always have to deal with ignorant people, and it's just a part of life. He says they're not important. It's the people who love you that count. If you're different too, it's going to be okay. You already have me as a friend and I love you this big (I'm stretching my arms out as far as they can go)!

*Autumn, you are a brave, beautiful soul. I bet you light up every room you walk into, like a great big bolt of sunshine. I'm so sorry about what happened in fifth grade. You were very brave to try again at a new school. I'd like to talk about your presentation. It was brilliant! Mrs. Baylor was right. Kids are afraid of what they don't understand. If you take away the mystery, it helps them to not to be scared anymore. What you and your mom did can work in many types of situations in which a student is visibly different.*

*For those of you listening who are struggling, maybe you're physically challenged or have a condition like Asperger's or Tourette's syndrome. Perhaps you have a birth defect or skin condition. Whatever your circumstance is, I'd like you to think about trying what Autumn and her mom did. Ask your parents to talk to the school principal with you. Tell your principal that you'd like to do a presentation to help your classmates understand a little more about you. Take time to put together the components of the presentation. Make sure you have photos and illustrations, and make it interesting and fun.*

*Most importantly, be open and honest. Don't be ashamed of whatever it is that makes you different. You are perfect and you are lovable the way you are. Give the other kids at school the chance to get to know you. And let them ask whatever questions they'd like. The more comfortable you are talking about yourself, the more comfortable they'll be getting to know you. If there's a funny story you want to share, go for it. If there's something important you want to say, say it. Don't hold back. Let the real you show through and be proud of who you are inside and out.*

*If you'd like some help getting started on your presentation, send me an e-mail. I'd be honored to walk you through the steps. Your parents can contact me too if they'd like. I know you're going to do great!*

## CHAPTER ELEVEN

# Hunter

I don't care what anyone says. You gotta stand up to bullies. Never ignore a bully. That doesn't mean you gotta go all apesh_t on someone, but if they mess with you, disrespect you, don't listen to that "leave them alone and they'll leave *you* alone" crap. That's being a bystander in your own friggin' life. I'm giving you the 411 and it's not from some book or boring assembly. I lived it sophomore year. Talk about a seriously messed up situation . . .

Hey, before I tell my story, I give you major props for being here. It's great you want to connect. I'm Hunter. I'm sixteen, but a very cool, *very* grown-up sixteen. I'm modest too! LOL. I'm from the city, not like the hood or anything, but a lot of the kids at my old school were. We had gangbangers, but they never bothered me or my friends. A couple of them saved my ass once. There was this group of assholes on the wrestling team who were threatening me over some stupid sh_t. This was outside the main building after last period, when these two bangers, I only knew them from study hall, saw what was going down, came over, and got me outta there. One of them got killed in a drive-by a couple of months later. His name was Troy. We got to be good friends. My parents and I went to his funeral. My throat hurt the whole time, like when you want to cry but you're trying to hold it in.

Gangbangers aren't all bad people. Some of these dudes, their only family is whatever gang they're in 'cause their real families are all f___ed up. They get sucked into the gang when they're little kids. I'm not saying it's okay what these dudes do to each other; it's *not* cool, okay? But they're not all stone-cold killers the way they make it sound on TV. It isn't that simple. Some of them, like Troy and Darius, he was the other guy who helped me that day, have had it rough. Sorry, I didn't mean to go there. It just pisses me off that life can be so unfair for some kids.

Anyway, back to my story. I pretty much got along with everyone but I had my own group of friends that I hung with, mostly skater dudes. It was cool. I kept my nose out of other people's sh_t, and they kept outta mine. I got into a couple of fights, totally stupid. Got suspended once for it for three days. I probably would have gotten a second suspension but Troy and Darius stopped that fight. My life wasn't perfect, but it was okay, until my parents started freaking out about my sister. I tried to get my parents to chill, but they were like, "We're moving."

My sister, Tamlyn, was fourteen. She's fifteen now. She was getting into hip-hop and rap, going totally "urban," and was crushing on some hardcore dudes. Darius told me these guys were into some heavy sh_t and to get her away from them. My parents had already been thinking about moving. After what Darius said, they got really scared. That same week, my sister tried to sneak out of the house with a fake ID. She was wearing so much makeup, and I hate to say this about my sis, but she looked like a reality show slut. Mom lost it when she found out what the fake ID was for. Tamlyn wanted a tattoo, and not one of those cute small ones, either. She wanted a big tat across her lower back. This dude at school, Caleb, told her she'd look hot with one and that he'd pay for it. Tamlyn got grounded for three weeks after Mom found out. The next morning, Mom called a real estate agent. By summer, we were "suburbanites."

I gotta admit, our new house was cool. Otto loved it. He's our dog, a rescue mutt. We got him when he was a puppy. He's old, like eleven, but we take really good care of him. When we go on vacations, my grandma and grandpa come and stay with him. He's a part of the family. He's got big, fuzzy ears and these short, fat little legs. He's really cute. The shelter said he's probably part Lab and Australian cattle dog. He's always trying to "herd" people. He pushes his head against your legs, and keeps pushing, until you go where he wants. Usually, it's into the kitchen next to the cabinet where Mom keeps his treat bowl. He's the third kid. He sleeps with my parents at night. Sometimes he'll sleep with Tamlyn or me, but he hangs with my mom the most. He follows her everywhere.

Okay, so, Tamlyn and me started at our new school. She was a freshman and I was a sophomore. The first day was a real trip. I never saw so many gangsta wannabes in my life. I wanted to say, yo dudes, you are *not* black from the inner city, you're *white* from the suburbs, and we *don't* need to see the cracks of your asses every day. Friggin' pull up your pants!

A group of them were hanging by the lockers, talking. They were wearing bling and trying to sound like "they was from the hood." F___ing hilarious. Darius would have busted a gut. Some other dude came up to me while I was watching them and goes, "I know, right?" I was like, "Are they serious?" He goes, "Wait, it gets better. You should see the chicks that hang with those guys." We both laughed.

His name was Reese. It was right before lunch period so he asked if I wanted to sit with him and his friends. I said, sure. They were pretty cool, not as edgy as the dudes I hung out with at my old school, but hey, it was all good. They were skaters too, so that was cool. After lunch, they invited me to hang out with them on Friday night. Tamlyn and I rode the school bus. On the ride home I asked her how her day went. She said she met this group of girls she really liked, and she was going to hang out with them on Saturday. She was psyched.

Everything was sweet for a while. Tamlyn made cheerleading. She ditched the whole inner-city hip-hop thing and was now totally into her Katy Perry thing. Even Otto was getting into the burbs. He dug the yard—get it, "dug" the yard, LMAO—anyway, he loved it. Mom and Dad had a fence installed, and he was a happy pup. I was hanging out with Reese and his group. Most weekends we were on our boards, or chilling at Reese's house. Then, the nightmare started.

There was this dude, Michael, a senior, sort of an outcast, real sketchy. A lot of people at school didn't like him. He was into all that anarchy sh_t, wore fatigues and combat boots, and had this dark, angry rap. Reese and those guys were afraid of him. A few times I caught him checking out Tamlyn. The way he was looking at her gave me the creeps.

I finally said something to him at lunch. He was sitting by himself. I told him to keep his perverted ass away from her. A bunch of kids sitting at the next table cracked up and gave me a high-five sign. As I was walking away, I could still hear them laughing at him and cutting him down. I almost felt sorry for him. He was one of those weird loner types. Sometimes, in the hallways, he'd give people the death stare.

After the thing with my sister, he started getting up in my face a lot. I was like, yeah, right, whatever dude. Then I started getting these weird text messages about "revenge" and "retribution." The number was blocked but I knew they were from him. It was like he had all this hatred for the world and needed someone to point it at, and that day at lunch, he picked me.

Reese goes, "You can't keep ignoring it." He thought I should kick Michael's ass. But school was going good and I didn't need a suspension. I knew some of the other kids thought I was being a total pussy. It sucked. Then someone started an anonymous rumor on Twitter that I was selling weed. Somebody's mom called the school, and the principal and two cops pulled me out of math class and searched my locker. Even though they didn't find anything, the school still had to call my parents. We tried to tell the principal it was Michael. He said he believed us, that Michael was on his radar, but he couldn't accuse a student without proof. We showed him all the text messages. Same problem. No friggin' proof.

The next day, Michael cornered me after gym class and went off about Tamlyn, telling me all this dirty, twisted sh_t he wanted to do to her. I lost it. A teacher had to pull me off of him. Michael and me were both suspended for three days. My parents and me met with the principal. I told him my side. He believed me that Michael started it, but because of zero tolerance, it didn't matter. He said he was gonna have a serious talk with Michael's dad, that "it was clear the boy needed help."

That night, my family started getting crank calls. At first they were stupid, like the kind little kids do. After a few days, they got darker. The caller said he was gonna burn down our house. The calls always came from an unknown number and whoever made them was using some voice changer app. We knew who it was. In the morning, my mom and dad went to Michael's house to try to talk to his parents. They wouldn't listen and his dad told my parents if they bothered them again, they were calling the cops. We went back to the principal. He said it happened off school property and there was nothing he could do. He told us to call the cops. We did. They told us to file a report, but until we had proof it was Michael, they couldn't do anything either. Two days later, my dad's car got vandalized in our driveway. We woke up and found all the tires slashed, and someone had spray-painted "f___ you" across the side of the car. We called the police again. They had us file another report. A couple of days later, Tamlyn and me got home from school, and found Otto in the yard, lying on his side, whimpering. He was barely moving. Tamlyn started to scream. I ran inside and got Mom. We wrapped Otto in a blanket and rushed him to the vet. We were all crying. I called Dad from the car. He must have driven a hundred miles an hour. He was standing outside the vet's office waiting when we got there. He helped us get Otto inside. The vet told us he would do everything he could. It was the longest four hours of my life. Mom prayed. Finally the vet came out and told us Otto would pull through. He wanted to keep him a couple of days to watch him, but he was gonna be okay. On the way out, the vet asked Dad if he could talk to him for a second in his office. Me and mom waited for him in the car. When Dad came out, his face was white. He told us that someone poisoned Otto. That night, he called a lawyer.

Everything happened pretty fast. The lawyer interviewed all our neighbors and asked them if they saw Michael hanging around anytime the day before. Two said they had, and one neighbor had a security camera that picked up Michael going into our yard. Our family pressed charges and we got a restraining order against him. Our lawyer got all over the school and the cops about these new laws in our state against bullying. My parents started an Anti-Bullying Action Committee and had a meeting at the village hall for people to sign up. Tons of people came. We had all this information about the new laws and what your rights are. We didn't want anyone to ever feel as helpless as we did.

That was a year ago. Now, the school has an anti-bullying task force, and they have lots of speakers come in to talk about bullying. In health class, they teach us about mental illness and the warning signs someone might be in trouble so we can report it. There was this one girl in my English class who some kids ended up reporting. She was cutting herself in the bathroom, and someone saw her notebook, and it was full of stuff about death. Her parents got her in a special hospital and she's doing better now.

Michael had to do community service, and then his family moved to another state. Every time I see a story on the news about some disturbed dude who goes on a shooting spree, there's a part of me that looks to see if it's him. If there's anyone at your school who acts angry all the time or who has a creepy, dark vibe, don't just make fun of him like a lot of the other kids, or ignore it. Tell the school to do something, anything, to help him, get him help, whatever. But *do* something.

*Your story is so important, Hunter. There's a lot we can learn from what you and your family went through. You're absolutely right that if you get a disturbing feeling about someone at school, if something just seems "off" about that person, report it to the administration. Don't wait. Do it immediately. You could be saving countless lives, including that of the tormented outcast.*

*I also want to discuss briefly when to hire a lawyer. Your dad did the right thing. He wasn't getting the level of responsiveness he needed from the school or the local authorities, and he enlisted an advocate. A lawyer can be very helpful, not only in standing up for you in a legal capacity, but she can educate you about your rights. New anti-bullying laws are being passed all the time, and a good attorney will know what the new laws are in your state and how to use them. Some law firms have specific experience in bullying cases. Just Google "law firms that specialize in school bullying" and dozens of sites pop up. Many of them are nonprofit organizations that can assist you in your search. If there's anyone listening who thinks it might help if your parents got a lawyer, be sure to research firms in your area specifically that have had success with bullying cases. You'll want someone who knows the terrain.*

*Lastly, too many people have died because a lonely, tormented outcast took revenge. Some of these shooters were mentally ill and slipped through the cracks. No one realized how sick they were. Others snapped because their illness took a turn for the worse or they skipped their meds. In both cases, there are warning signs. If someone threatens violence, take it seriously. If someone fantasizes about retribution or shows an unusual interest in death or destruction, if someone laughs at suffering, or seems to delight in having others fear them, listen to your intuition. Step up and say something. Make yourself heard.*

# CHAPTER TWELVE

# Riley

[*Recording*]

Testing, testing, one, two, three.

Testing, testing.

My Story by Riley.

Hi! I'm Riley. I'm fourteen. Tina is my best friend. *Hi Tina!* My hair is short. I look like a boy. I'm a girl. I like cargo shorts and boy's sweatshirts. I'm tall. I have blue eyes. Mom said I could wear eye shadow if I want. Yuck, no way!

Um, I get mad a lot. I feel sad a lot too. Sometimes I hear voices. They tell me to do bad things. The doctor says they aren't real. I have to take medicine so they'll be quiet. Sometimes the medicine doesn't work.

I have mental illness. I know because my mom and the doctors said. Mom says to never feel ashamed. She says some kids have to take medicine 'cause of stuff like diabetes or asthma. I have to take medicine for when I don't feel good inside my head. I have bipolar disorder. Mine is more harder because of the voices. Lucky me, LOL. I have OCD too. It makes me do things over and over and I can't stop.

I'm thirsty. I'll be right back.

[Pause]

[*Recording*]

Okay, I'm back. I give lots of hugs. When I see someone I love, I run up to them and hug them as hard as I can. That way, if they go away like my dad, I just close my eyes really tight and remember the hugs, and it's like they're there again. I have to be careful 'cause sometimes when I get too excited I knock people down when I hug them. It's pretty funny.

Um, what else . . . oh yeah, I know! I'm on volleyball. I'm the best player. Tina's on volleyball too. Our team made state.

I pull out my hair sometimes. Mom's made me a see a ton of doctors about it. It's 'cause of the OCD. When it gets really bad, I wear a baseball cap to school to hide it. I started cutting too. Mom doesn't know about that part. I only told Tina. I use a paperclip. I open it all the way up and use the end of it on my arms and legs. I dig it into my skin.

I don't feel like talking anymore right now.

[Stop]

[*Recording*]

Hi. It's been a couple days. A lot's been going on. Tina told Mom about the cutting. Mom freaked out. I started pulling out my hair again. Mom took me to more doctors. They changed my medicine. The new medicine makes me feel funny. I almost hit my little brother. I locked myself in my room and banged my head against the wall. I kept doing it for a long time. I had to have stitches. Mom is taking me to another doctor tomorrow. He says we'll need to change my medicine again. Mom doesn't want me to go back to school until my medicines are fixed. I don't want to miss volleyball practice. Mom says the other kids won't understand about my hair. I have big bald spots.

I'm tired. I'm gonna go to bed. I'll talk more tomorrow. G'night.

[Stop]

[*Recording*]

Today was the worst. Seth snuck up behind me at lunch for no reason and pulled my baseball cap off. Seth is always mean to me. I tried to cover the bald spots with my hands, but I couldn't. Everybody was laughing. Then, this girl, Ally, said I had cancer. All day people kept looking at me. Some kids wanted to know if I was going to die. I went to the bathroom and started pulling out my hair again. These girls walked in. One of them said, "OMG, she's not sick, she's just *mental*!" She started texting. I ran out. On the way to class, someone pushed me down the stairs. My arm got broke and my finger. Mom had to take me to the emergency room.

We just got home. Mom's on the phone with the principal. I'm so tired.

I'm going to watch TV now.

TTYL.

[Stop]

[*Recording*]

Hi. It's me, Riley. The cast is off. My finger is way better too. I didn't mean to go away for so long. I'm sorry. Please don't be mad at me. The voices came back. They were really bad. Mom had to put me in a hospital. That's where I am now. It's been a whole month. I hate it here. The doctors and nurses are mean. There are too many rules. They won't let you have hardly anything in your room. They found a paperclip in my stuff and I lost two privileges. No phone and no iPod for two days. That's what they do when you break one of their dumb rules. You lose privileges. The nurses check the rooms all the time. One kid couldn't watch TV for a day 'cause he didn't turn his belt in when he got here. There are fifteen other kids in my ward. I share a room with this one girl, Ocean. Her parents met on a beach. That's how she got that name. She has bipolar too. She tried to drink poison. She's here 'cause of that.

The doctors make all us kids do therapy. We have activities too. I like drama and music time. Art is kind of boring. Some kids have to take a lot of medicine. It makes their eyes all dead. I hate taking medicine. The doctors never get it right.

I want to go home.

[Stop]

[*Recording*]

This place sucks. It's seven weeks now. Why won't they just let me go home? I'm better. I am. I told Mom I wouldn't pull out my hair anymore. No more cutting too. Please, I just want to go home. I want to go home. I want to go home! I hate the doctors. They make me talk about stuff I don't want to. They're mean. They're like aliens from another planet, the *Mean* Planet. I hate them. I hate everyone. The food here is gross. It smells like feet. I can't stand it. Tell Mom to get me out of here. Tell her. Mom, please, please, *please.* I want to go home.

She can't hear me.

No one can hear me.

Uh-oh, the nurse is coming. I gotta go. I have to hide my paperclip. Yeah, I still have one. So what? It's just a paperclip. Wanna know where I keep it so no one will find it? At night I wear a mouth guard 'cause I grind my teeth. I keep my paperclip inside the case. Hah!

The nurse just came in. I'll be back in a minute. Wait, why is she looking at my retainer case?

[Pause]

[*Recording*]

She found it. I bet Ocean told her. No phone privileges for three days! I hate this place. Now I can't call Tina on her birthday.

God?

It's me, Riley. Please let me go home. Please, I'll be good, cross my heart and hope to die, stick a needle in my eye! I won't get in trouble. I promise I won't hurt myself anymore. I won't be mean to my brother and sister. God, please, just let me go home. Please, I'm better now. Please . . .

I hope He heard me. I closed my eyes and everything.

Hey, I got a letter from my dad today! He says he's going to visit me. Yay!

I better get going. But isn't that cool about my dad?

[Stop]

[*Recording*]

It's me again. One of the kids in my ward today was screaming real bad. The nurses had to hold him. They gave him a shot. He went to sleep. His mom and dad are here now. They look scared. Ocean said he's way sicker than the rest of us. She said some kids have to live here forever like jail. They *never* get to go home. I scream sometimes. God, please don't let that happen to me.

[Stop]

[*Recording*]

No fair! Ocean went home today.

[Stop]

[*Recording*]

It's over two months and I'm *still* here. Tina came to visit me today. I didn't feel like talking to her. I don't want to talk to anyone.

[Stop]

[*Recording*]

Mom brought me new batteries for my tape recorder. She says I have to go to a special school in the fall. At least that means I'll get out of the hospital soon. I can't stand it anymore.

[Stop]

[*Recording*]

Hi again. Dad's coming today! I'm *so* excited! I haven't seen him in a whole year. He has a new family. My sister says he doesn't like our old one anymore. I can't believe he's going to visit me! Last time he yelled at me a lot. I made him a special poster this time. I taped pictures of all his favorite things on it. It was hard to make 'cause there's no scissors here. I tore out the pictures from old magazines in the book room. I used a ruler to hold down the page and then I tore the pictures out one at a time. I had to be really careful or the whole page would rip. I wish I had scissors but it looks okay. I hope he likes it and doesn't yell at me again. I got pictures of fishing, and cars, and trees, and I even found a picture of a chocolate brownie.

I better go. I want to be ready when he gets here. Yay!

TTYL.

[Pause]

[*Recording*]

Dad isn't here yet. He was supposed to be here at one o'clock. It's two o'clock plus fifteen minutes. I want to call his cell, but the stupid nurse won't let me. I lost my phone privileges again. It wasn't 'cause of another paperclip thing. I took a pen from the reception desk. I hid it in my pillowcase. I wasn't gonna cut myself with it. I wasn't!

Where are you, Dad!?

[Pause]

[*Recording*]

It's four o'clock. The nurse is calling him now. She's leaving him a voicemail . . .

[Pause]

[*Recording*]

Dinner just finished. I didn't eat anything. I'm too worried. Besides, it was meatloaf and green beans. Totally gross. Dad still isn't here. Dear God, please let him be okay.

[Pause]

[*Recording*]

Dad isn't coming.

[Stop]

[*Recording*]

He didn't come. He called at ten o'clock and said he couldn't make it. I guess my sister is right. Maybe Mom will find a new dad for us. A lot of kids don't like getting a new dad or a new mom and they're mean about it. I'd never be mean. I want a dad again so bad, I'd be the best daughter ever so he'd like me and wouldn't go away.

I have to go to bed. You get in trouble if you stay up past lights out. You get in trouble for anything here.

See you tomorrow.

[Stop]

[*Recording*]

Riley's home! This is Tina. She wanted me to say hi. I'm so happy to get my best friend back! I missed her *so* bad. We're gonna go play volleyball at the park. Riley says she'll talk to you later. Nice meeting you!

[Stop]

[*Recording*]

Hi, it's Riley again. Isn't Tina awesome! We've been hanging out a lot since I got back. That's the good news. The bad news is Mom has all these new rules at our house. I can't lock my bedroom door. I have to be "respectful" of others. No more hiding stuff. If I start cutting again, I have to tell my mom right away. There are a ton of other rules too. If I break any, I lose a privilege, just like at the stupid hospital. It sucks but I'm still glad to be home. Sorry I can't talk longer. Mom's dropping me off at the mall to meet Tina. We're going shopping for school clothes.

I'm scared to start at my new school. Tina says I have to be brave. I'll try. At least I still have a month left of summer.

[Stop]

[*Recording*]

Hi! You won't believe what happened. It's *so* cool. The pastor at our church started a club for bullied kids and he asked me to be one of the junior leaders! I started a week ago and I really like it. When I'm older, I want to work with kids like me who have had to go through a lot.

There's this one girl in the club, Michaela. She's going into third grade. Her dad is in jail. Everybody in the neighborhood knows, and the kids at school were really mean to her last year. No one would play with her at recess. They made fun of her on the bus and put hair in her food at lunch. Someone left a big dead bug in her backpack. Her mom changed schools. She starts a new one when summer's over. She's scared. I've been giving her lots of hugs and doing fun things with her. Tina and I told her we're her new big sisters. We've been giving her volleyball lessons. Mom took her to see the new Muppet movie with us (I *love* the Muppets). This week our club went to the zoo, and then a concert for kids at the beach, and we helped at a food drive. Michaela told me today that she's not as scared to start school. She said she loved me and that I was the best big sister ever. When I told Mom, she was so happy.

[Stop]

[*Recording*]

Hi, it's Riley. School starts tomorrow. I wish I could go to the normal school with Tina. She just went home. We hung out all day. I cried when she left. She said we're best friends forever, and it doesn't matter we won't be at the same school. She said we're still gonna hang out all the time just like always. I hope she doesn't get a new best friend. Okay, I better go. Wish me luck for tomorrow.

[Stop]

[*Recording*]

Hi, sorry it's so late. I wanted to wait until Mom went to bed before I started recording. Today was my official first day of high school. Mom drove me but after tomorrow, I have to take the bus. There are only twelve freshmen including me at the whole school. This one girl had a pierced lip and purple and orange hair. She had on tons of black eyeliner, and her nails were polished black. She came over to talk to me. Her name was Jade. She was kind of nice. We made friends.

Lunch was weird. It's not like at my other school where you sit wherever you want. At the new school, you sit with your class. I sat next to Jade. Every table has a teacher, too. At our table, it's the math teacher. He kind of looks like Brad Pitt. Jade says he's her new "secret crush." He says math should be fun, and if it's not, it's the teacher's fault. He is the coolest adult ever.

[Stop]

[*Recording*]

I can't believe it's Halloween already. Michaela came over with her mom for trick-or-treat. She looked so cute. She was Elmo! She even had the giggle down. She says she likes school. Her mom thanked me for helping her.

I gotta go. Jade's here. She and Tina and me are going to Starbucks. Mom's driving us. We were gonna go trick-or-treating, but we decided that's kid stuff. See ya later!

[Stop]

[*Recording*]

Sorry I haven't recorded in a while. I've been super busy with school and my friends. Jade is really cool and she hangs out a lot with Tina and me. Tina really likes her. Michaela's mom dropped her off at my house tonight. Her mom has some meeting, and we're watching her. She's gonna be in the Christmas pageant at school. She's playing a sheep. Mom says she'll take Tina and Jade and me to see it.

I better do my homework now.

TTYL.

[Stop]

[*Recording*]

I don't really feel like talking. I just wanted to tell you what happened. I finally saw Dad. I spent the weekend at his house with his new family. I've only met my stepmom three times. She's like a stranger. She's kind of uptight. She gets all nervous when I'm around the new baby. Oh yeah, my dad's got a baby with her. The weekend was okay until I screwed up. I made microwave popcorn and I put it in the good bowl instead of the plastic popcorn bowl. I dropped it and it broke. Dad's wife went ballistic. She started yelling. Dad started yelling. The baby woke up. It was crying and wouldn't stop. Dad said, "I f___ing hope *this* kid isn't a waste like you."

I called Mom and told her to pick me up. She felt so bad for me. She wanted to say something to Dad. What's the point? He is who he is. That's okay. Tomorrow will be better.

G'night.

[Stop]

[*Recording*]

Yep, me again! I had a good day at school. I made friends with this new kid Jonah. He doesn't have a dad either. Jonah was in the same hospital before as me. We talked about this one nurse who looked just like the librarian from *Monsters, Inc.* She sounded like her too. Whenever she did room checks, she talked to herself, like whole conversations. She'd ask herself a question and then answer it. Jonah said, "Yeah, and *we* were the ones who were supposed to be crazy, LOL."

Oh wait, Tina's texting me. Later, alligator.

That was Riley's last recording. It's me, Tina. Six days ago my best friend shot herself. Her mom came home from the grocery store and found her dead. Her uncle had an antique gun collection. He kept it locked in a case in the attic. Riley found the key. I feel bad for her uncle. He blames himself, but it's not his fault. I knew her better than anyone. If she couldn't have gotten her uncle's gun, she would have done something else. Riley died before she killed herself. She started getting sick again around Christmas. She was pulling out her hair and cutting herself worse than ever. Her mom thought maybe something bad happened at school. Riley wouldn't talk about it, not even to me. Her mom was going to put her back in the hospital after Christmas.

Riley was *so* full of life. Her hugs were like vitamins. She *wanted* to live but the voices in her head said no. Most people leave a suicide note. Riley left a thank-you note. She thanked every single person in her life for loving her. She said to everyone to please not be mad at her, but that the voices wanted her to go to heaven now.

Her funeral was last night. The whole town came to say goodbye. Everyone from her church, the kids from her youth group and all their parents and friends, everyone from school. Over a thousand people showed up. Michaela drew a picture of her and Riley and me playing volleyball. She said she and her mom were going to tie it to a big helium balloon, and write the word "heaven" on it, so that when she let it go into the sky, Riley would find it. Riley would have loved that.

I saw Seth at the funeral. You remember him, the jerk who pulled Riley's baseball cap off that day at lunch. He said he saw her at the mall with Jade right before she died. He said he was with a bunch of kids from school. One of them started making fun of her, calling her a "mental case." He said Jade got all up in the guy's face and told him to f___ off. By then, he said everyone at Starbucks was staring at them. "I didn't make fun of her that day," he said. "I told the dude to leave her alone, but he wouldn't." He started to cry. He asked me if it was their fault she killed herself. I wanted to say, *YES! You and your stupid friends bullied her every day! Don't think I don't know it was YOU who pushed her down the stairs! Yes, you and everyone else at school killed Riley and I hope you all rot in hell for it!* I didn't. It was mental illness that killed my friend.

The only thing that bothers me is this. When someone is sick like Riley, it's like they've got two groups of bullies, the voices in their head, and the bullies at school. I wonder if someone would have stopped the bullies at school, if maybe the bullies in Riley's head wouldn't have been so mean to her.

I love you, Riley.

*Hi, Tina. I wonder the same thing. I remember how hard it was being bullied and I didn't have to cope with the pain and isolation of mental illness. Riley was the bravest girl I ever knew. She brought so much love and light into the world. I miss her too, with all my heart.*

*I'd like to take a moment to talk about self-harm and mental illness. Tina, I know how hard it must have been for you to tell Riley's mom about her cutting. Riley was angry with you for a little while, but you did the right thing. For anyone who's listen-*

ing now, if you know someone who's cutting or hurting themselves in any way, you MUST tell an adult. Do it NOW. I know you may be afraid the person you tell on will be mad at you, but sometimes you have to risk a friendship to save a life. In the end, if that person is truly your friend, she'll know you did it for her own good, that you loved her enough to let her be mad at you so you could help her. That's why Tina was such a good friend. She loved Riley for who she was, she accepted her illness, and she was strong enough to face her fear of Riley's anger to prevent her from hurting herself more. Tina represents what a best friend truly should be. Riley was blessed to have her.

One last but VERY important subject I want to address—suicide. If you know anyone who's having suicidal thoughts, or if YOU think about it sometimes, it is NEVER the answer. You never know what joys life has waiting for you just around the corner. Please, don't hide in silence, whether it's you or someone you know. Speak up. Tell an adult. Get help and support. Here's a phone number you can call to talk with a caring adult— 1-800-273-TALK (8255). You ARE loved.

Riley, if you're listening, you are loved so very much.

# CHAPTER THIRTEEN

# Aaron

I wanted to belong. I didn't mean to hurt anyone. I could have blown my whole future. I'm Aaron. Hi. I'm a senior. Thanks for hanging with me. You know in those commercials where someone is doing some crazy stunt, and in little letters across the bottom of your TV screen, it says, "Do not attempt." Pretend you're reading that here, and *do not attempt* what I did. Seriously, for someone as smart as me, I did something really stupid. I was lonely and desperate, not a good combo.

I got the memo in elementary school—I was "different." In third grade we had to do this dumb spelling bee. I never had to sound out any of the words. I just "knew" how to spell them. The other kids thought I cheated. Even some of their parents thought that. I learned how to read when I was three. If I read something once it's like my brain locks it in and I can remember the words. I never had to count with my fingers, either. Most math problems I can do in my head. The other kids thought I was weird. They teased me and put me down all the time. Every day it was something new—the T-shirt I had on, what I ate for lunch, how I held a pencil, it didn't matter. Mom said it was because they were jealous of me. Inside I'd scream, *Who cares about WHY everyone is mean to me. Just make them like me! I hate grownups. All they do is explain, explain, EXPLAIN but nothing ever gets better!* My parents are a whole other story. I'll tell you about them later.

I wanted to fit in so bad at school. Sometimes when I did someone's homework or let them look at my answers during a quiz, they'd let me play with them at recess. That didn't work after fifth grade. Middle school was harsh. The teachers didn't help either. They'd be handing back a paper or a test, and when they got to mine, they'd hold it up in front of everyone, and say, "Look at Aaron's work. Now *this* is how it's done!" My English teacher would read my essays out loud to the entire class, then say, "See what you can do if you put your mind to it like Aaron!" I wanted to hide under the desk. If there are any teachers listening in, please don't do stuff like that. It's hard enough for certain kids already.

Things got worse after Dad made me take some stupid IQ test. It said I was in the "gifted" range. That test ruined my life. He thought it would make me feel better about myself. It only made me feel worse. It was like proof on paper that I would never be normal. At least some of the kids in the honor roll society had been okay to me up until then. They never invited me to hang out with them but they said hi sometimes, and if there was an empty seat at their table at lunch, they'd let me sit there. They must have found out about my test score, probably thanks to my parents bragging on Facebook, because they stopped talking to me.

I thought high school would be better. I found out being "gifted" was no f___ing gift. I always had to be better than everyone else at everything I did, or my parents gave me sh_t. I was never proud of being smarter than some of the other kids; I was ashamed. I never asked to be "above average" or "gifted." It's all BS anyway. What makes a person special is who they are inside, not some random number. Courage without genius can change the world. Genius without courage doesn't mean sh_t. Try telling that to my dad. It sucked always having to live up to his expectations. Like freshman year, I got an A on my first high-school science paper, and he was disappointed it wasn't an A+. It was a really hard paper, and I was the *only* freshman in the whole school to score above a C. He said, "Son, you could have done better."

If God would have come down to my room that day and said, "Aaron, listen, I'll make you a deal. You don't have to be gifted anymore, but you'll only live until graduation," I would have said, "Okay, I'll take it." I was so lonely, I'd rather have had four years of feeling normal and happy with friends and a social life than a lifetime of more misery. My parents didn't get it. They didn't want to. In their minds, their son was special and the unfortunate peons of this world would just have to deal with it.

Being an only child didn't help either. Even when I was in kindergarten, long before Dad shoved that f___ing IQ test down my throat, they needed me to be better than everyone. The teacher said to bring a bath towel for naptime. Know what my parents did instead? They had a rug *custom*-made with dopey little bells on it that spelled out my name. All the kids laughed at me and I got in trouble for not listening to directions. Plus, the bells jingled and no one could nap!

My dad was the high-school quarterback and he got a full ride to college. Freshman year, he blew out his knee and dropped out. He got a job working for a carpenter, and that's what he does now, carpentry work. He hates his job. He's always saying he should have been CEO of a tech company and not pounding nails in other people's houses. Ever since I was born, he put all this pressure on me, constantly telling me not to make the same mistakes he did. If I did make a mistake, he'd say he could accept it if I were "average," but with my "gifts," there's no excuse for screwing up. It's like he made *me* responsible for living out *his* hopes and dreams. I'd try to talk to him about it, but he wouldn't listen. He'd say everything he did was for my own good and if I couldn't see that, I was the jerk, not him.

By my sophomore year, school was so bad that I started pretending I was a soldier going off to war every day. I started watching war movies like *Black Hawk Down* to get through the worst of it. The thing about high school, and you probably know this already, is that once you're branded "the outcast," you're stuck with it. Makeovers are for reality shows, not real life.

The thing I hated most was when teachers called on me in class. I was f___ed no matter what. If I answered wrong on purpose, it hurt my grade and the teacher would embarrass me in front of everyone, saying he expected "more" from me, but when I answered right, the other kids thought I was sucking up or showing off, and it made them bully me more. It wasn't just one or two bullies either. Everyone messed with me. Someone would start teasing me, and then another person would get in on the fun, and then another. Sometimes I wondered if they were bonding over my pain. I swear to God, it was like this show on Animal Planet that I saw once about "the pack mentality." They were the wolves and I was their prey.

I went to my parents for help. I know, I know. I had a weak moment. They said to "ignore the bullies" and "focus on my future," and that in twenty years I'd be famous and successful and the bullies would be nowhere in life. I *didn't care* about the future. I cared about the weekend and not wanting to be alone again, pissed off and depressed.

Finally, I couldn't take it anymore. I told my parents I wanted a fresh start at a new school. At first they wanted me to tough it out. But when I got off the bus one day wet and muddy with no books and my parents asked me where my backpack was, and I said at the bottom of Papoose Lake where a bunch of kids held me down, grabbed it, and threw it into the water, they changed their minds. They couldn't afford private school. My dad made too much money for financial aid, but not enough to make the tuition. They talked to the superintendent of my school and he said I could go to the other high school in the district. I'd have to get up way earlier for the bus, but it would be all different kids and I could have the fresh start I wanted. We decided I'd finish out sophomore year where I was, and in the fall I'd start my junior year at the new school.

Over the summer I came up with a plan. I figured a fresh start only counted if I changed who I was; otherwise, I'd be an outcast again. I got a job mowing lawns so I'd have enough money to make it work. I had to be convincing. I went to all the cool stores at the mall and got some hipster jeans, some cool shirts, and killer Nikes that everyone was wearing. It's kind of weird but I did feel cooler about myself after. I used to wear boring jeans and T-shirts. My new stuff was way different. When I showed it to my parents, they were like, OMG, but they figured if it makes me more psyched about school, okay, fine.

I don't want to bore you with all the details, but let's just say my plan worked great until report cards came out, and then everything got all f___ed up. Here's what I did. I screwed up stuff on purpose so the other kids would see how cool and normal I was. When the teachers would call on me, I'd either give a totally wrong answer, or I'd act like a jerk and say something funny to impress everyone. At first it was really hard doing a whole makeover of my personality. It felt weird knowing an answer and faking dumb. Most people did the opposite. But it was so great not having teachers expect me to be their perfect example all the time. It felt so good being wrong; it was like total, awesome freedom. It's hard to explain, but as my grades went to sh_t, and teachers got more and more disgusted with my "attitude," I was happier. The other kids weren't mean to me like before. They thought I was cool and funny. I got invited to parties and it was like the ultimate, best ever, fantasy come true. I finally got to know what it felt like to fit in.

For a couple of months, life was f___ing sweet. Then reality hit. The school sent my parents a letter saying they were concerned because I'd gone from straight As at my last school, to Cs and Ds at their school, and that I was "acting up" in class. My parents went off on me. I told them the truth. They couldn't understand why such a "gifted" kid would screw up his future like that, just to be a part of the "cool" crowd. It was like I betrayed them. That was the whole problem. I was their life. They needed to have their own. I tried to make them understand. They wouldn't. They couldn't. Dad said either I get my grades back up, or else. I picked "or else." They tried grounding me. I'd sneak out of the house if there was a party. They tried bribing me with a car. I said I didn't need one. They tried begging. I was like, "whatever."

My junior year was hell for my parents, but I figured my whole life had been hell for me, and I was sort of like, "Payback's a bitch." Then, one night, I saw Mom crying in the kitchen. I asked her what was wrong. She said she and Dad were sorry for pushing me so hard, that they know they should have let me be a normal kid sometimes, and it was their fault everything was such a mess. That got to me. It's not like I didn't know what I was doing was wrong, but I couldn't make myself care because I liked having friends. The one thing I didn't think about was college. I hadn't even registered for SATs yet and I'd have to start applying to schools in the fall. The earlier you apply, the better your chance of getting a scholarship. It was already almost the end of spring semester. Honestly, I wasn't thinking past the weekends. My parents were freaking. I was freaking now too. I hurt them. I didn't mean to. I was just tired of living in the "gifted" prison.

They sat me down and said, "Look, you've got to tell the kids at school the truth, let them know who you really are, not this fake version of you. If they're really your friends by now, they'll still like you." I was scared sh_tless but I knew they were right. That Saturday night, I spilled. I was waiting to be laughed at or spat on. I started getting flashbacks from my old school. I think I might have been crying, but I'm not sure. I was too scared to know what I was doing. Then, this girl Emory came up to me and hugged me. She said she couldn't believe I would go through so much for their friendship, that they would still think I'm cool even if I got answers right and made straight As. Who I am inside, she said, is why they all liked me. It was a shock. I know I did cry then because a bunch of the guys came up and said, "Whoa dude, chill, it's all good." Then, someone said, "Now that we know you're smart, can we cheat off you? Only kidding, LOL." Everyone laughed and it felt like the world changed in that moment. When I got home, I told my parents what happened. It was the first time I ever felt close to them. They said they were more proud of me than they ever were before.

The only thing was college. I'd never seen Dad look so sad. He knew he couldn't afford tuition. A scholarship was my only chance, and after what I'd pulled, it looked like that was out. I was lucky I hadn't missed the deadline for SATs. I studied with my friends and we all did really well on the test. None of us had to take it again.

Fast-forward to the beginning of this year. I applied to a bunch of colleges. The rejection letters were harder on my parents than me. They still blamed themselves for causing my "rebellion," and now they were afraid it was going to screw up the rest of my life. Then, I got a thick envelope in the mail. If you haven't applied to college yet, you'll find this out. Skinny envelopes are rejections and the thick ones are acceptance packages. I got waitlisted at NYU. That was my first pick because I wanted to go to their business school. Mom suggested I be proactive and write them a letter explaining what happened. I did. The head of admissions called and said he couldn't get me into the business school. He tried, but he gave my letter to the head of admissions for a special program for gifted writers. It was a two-year liberal arts school within the university, and if I did well there, I could do an internal transfer my junior year into the business school. He said my letter blew a lot of people away at NYU, and that if I took him up on his offer, they would make some scholarship money available. But I had to promise one thing. That senior year, I would "kick ass with my grades." Yes, sir!

Two weeks later Mom, Dad, and I were on a plane to New York for my admissions interview. It was the last step before I could officially be accepted. The professor who interviewed me was really nice. She said when she read my letter, she cried because her granddaughter was being bullied at school. We talked for a long time and she asked me lots of questions. Then, she handed me a Freshman Orientation folder, and said, "Welcome to NYU." My parents and I celebrated that night in New York at this amazing restaurant in Greenwich Village. That's where NYU is. It's the most awesome neighborhood. You should see my dorm! It's off Washington Square Park, which is this amazing place where people come and hang out and musicians play guitars and sing. I know I'm going to love college. Another few months, then graduation, and then New York!

Before I go, there's something I want to say. I was lucky. My story could have ended up way different. I hurt my parents and myself, and almost screwed up my whole future. If there's someone at your school who's "gifted," give that person a chance. Don't do to them what the kids did to me. If you're the one who's being bullied, I know it sucks, but you don't have to invent a new you to make friends. You don't have to change schools either. Find something not connected to school that you can join where you'll meet new people. The park district has tons of stuff and so do a lot of local libraries and community centers. It's better if it's in a different neighborhood from where you live so it'll be a fresh start with kids you don't already go to school with. If I had to do everything over again, I would have tried that first and not lied to everyone, including myself, about who I was and what I really wanted. I almost didn't get into college because of it. Like I said, I was lucky.

*Aaron, I'm glad you're here. A lot of people think if you're gifted in any way, you're less likely to be bullied or excluded. You know firsthand that's not true. I'm happy things turned out well for you, but your advice is right on target. You were one of the lucky ones. Living a lie might work for a little while, as it did for you, but eventually, the truth will out. When it does, you have no control. If you're going through what Aaron did, and wish you could be anyone other than who you are, hang in there. Don't dumb yourself down or put on a phony act. Find someplace where you can be you in peace. Ask your parents or a teacher to help you research activities for teens near you, and reach out into the world to find where you belong. Be proud of who you are, not ashamed. You're a bright light. Shine, don't hide!*

*If there are any teachers listening in, Aaron isn't the only student I've heard complain about educators who cite them as examples of excellence. I know you mean well, that you see it as a form of encouragement. You're thinking like an adult. If you really want to understand this from the kid's point of view, you have to think in his or her age. What the kid thinks as the teacher sings his praises in front of everyone is, "Dear God, just kill me now." Better to compliment the student privately. Otherwise, you're setting him up as a potential target of bullies.*

# CHAPTER FOURTEEN

# Gemma

I'm Gemma. I'm in eighth grade. It's boring and it sucks but whatever. I feel uncomfortable talking to you. I pretend to be all open with people, but I never really let anyone get inside. I did up until middle school, and then everything got messed up and I didn't care about anyone anymore.

Today totally freaked me out! This thing happened at school that changed everything and I wasn't sure I could even talk about it, but if I don't, I'll probably just feel worse.

Okay, so, I'm in eighth grade. Oh yeah, I already said that. Sorry. Anyway, this morning Jodee came to speak at my school. I never even heard of her before. I was *so* not into it. Most people are BS. And she was like the queen of everything I hated. She was like super pretty, and in my head I was like, "Yeah, right, bitch, like *you* were bullied. You are *so* full of sh_t! The only reason you're telling this phony story is to sell your stupid book."

I f___ing hated her, but like my BFFs were totally into her whiny crap so I had to pretend to give a sh_t. Jodee cried sometimes in the talk. I still thought she was full of it.

Then she told this story about how when she was in fifth grade, her friends turned on her 'cause she was her own person and didn't want to make fun of kids just because everyone else was. That like freaked me *so* out 'cause the same thing happened to me in fifth grade. So I thought maybe I should give her a chance. I really listened to the rest of her talk. Then afterward, me and my friends went up to her. We asked her if we could talk to her alone. She was really nice about it. She hugged me and said she knew what it was like to be bullied. I go, "No, I'm not bullied. OMG, me and my friends are like the most popular clique at school." She asked what was wrong. I told her about this kid, Eric. He was the school outcast. Ever since fifth grade, we were really mean to him. I told Jodee me and my friends were wondering if she could help us figure out how to make it up to him. We wanted to tell him we were sorry. Jodee got us a classroom and told the principal to bring Eric down.

Okay, so, before I tell you the rest of the story, this is the kind of stuff we did to Eric. I'm not proud of it, but I promised if I talked to you, I'd tell the truth. I think I'm gonna throw up.

Okay, so Eric was a weird dude. He was like mental. He'd make all these weird sounds all the time, and he could never look you in the eye. I'm just saying the dude was like retarded. So me and my friends did this thing where we'd wait until right before the second bell rang when Eric was passing our math class on his way to homeroom, and we'd bang the erasers against the chalkboard really hard. It made this super loud popping sound like a gun. Eric would *freak out*. He'd start crying and screaming and a few times he pissed his pants. My friends and I would high-five each other. Like I said, I'm not proud of it, okay? It was stupid and mean, what we did. I don't even know why we got off on it so much.

Okay, so we were hanging out in the classroom with Jodee when the principal came in and said Eric was waiting in the hall. He asked if we were ready. Jodee went out to talk to Eric for a minute alone first. I kind of was wishing I'd never started this. There were about fifteen of us "bullies" in the room, mostly cheerleaders and guys on the basketball team. Our school was a total jock school. The basketball team won state championships three years in a row.

Jodee came back in with Eric. He whispered something in her ear. She said, "Okay." Then he went to the front of the room and said he wasn't mad at us for being mean, that he knew he was weird. He said it was 'cause he had this thing called Asperger's. He said it made it hard for him to talk to people and look them in the eye and stuff. He said that he could think okay, that he wasn't dumb or anything, but that a part of his brain was broken and he couldn't help it when he got all spastic. I felt bad. He was being sweet and we were always jerks to him. I remember this one time at lunch we put soap in his food. He had to go to the nurse's office. How could we have been that awful?

Okay, so—I say that when I'm nervous. I start every sentence with "okay, so." My mom says it's a bad habit, but like, I'm so nervous right now that I just want to keep saying "okay, so" over and over, until you get sick of it and I don't have to talk anymore. Me and my friends f___ed up. It was the kind of mistake that a person has to live with forever, like drunk drivers when they hit someone.

Eric said, "You know how when you banged the erasers real loud against the chalkboard, and I'd scream and sometimes have a accident, but it wasn't 'cause of my Asperger's; it was 'cause of something else."

I think praying is dumb, but I said a prayer then.

"I scream 'cause when I was in fourth grade, my mom went to the store and left me home with my dad, and I was nervous 'cause of the cartoon on TV, 'cause the roadrunner was being mean to the coyote again, and the coyote was hurt bad, and the roadrunner kept saying, 'beep, beep' and I blocked my ears, but the roadrunner wouldn't stop, and I started making popping sounds, 'pop, pop, pop' with my finger in my mouth, and my dad told me to stop, and I couldn't, and he kept telling me he was sick of having a retard son, and then he yelled at me and I was screaming, and he got his gun, and he put it next to his head, and he shot it, and there was blood all over and it got on the TV, and I screamed, and then I was in the hospital."

I looked over at my friends. None of us knew what to say. Jodee was holding Eric's hand. The principal was guarding the door.

"That's how come I scream when I hear the erasers," Eric said. "They sound like Daddy's gun, and I think it's going to be all blood everywhere again."

I wanted to die. I got up and hugged Eric. I told him over and over how sorry I was for being such a bitch to him. He said, "It's okay, Gemma, don't cry." I felt so small. By then, my friends had gotten up and were coming over. We all gave Eric a group hug. We stayed like that for a really long time. It was lunch period, so the principal had food brought up. The counselor came too to make sure we were all okay. She asked if there was something us kids could do for Eric to "say we're sorry in actions and not just words." Eric got all red, and said, "I want to learn how to play basketball." The guys all volunteered to play with him after school twice a week before practice, and we invited him to sit with us at lunch every day, and we're going to include him in lots of cool stuff. He's part of the gang now. It's not 'cause of guilt. It's not. We found out that Eric is cool in his own special way.

He changed all of us.

Okay, so (I know I'm doing it again, sorry), I *never* talk about this but if Eric could be brave, I will too. There was another reason I wanted to be friends with Eric after what happened. He's my hero now. I know I'm a bitch. I never give a sh_t about anyone. I like making fun of people and laughing at them. It makes me feel important I guess. Here's the thing. I wasn't always a terrible person. In elementary school, I was nice. I stuck up for people and if someone was being mean, I got up in their face. Like there was this one kid, Adam. By fifth grade he already knew what he wanted to be when he grew up. He wanted to be a radio talk show host. It was so weird 'cause nobody even knew what that was. He had these ugly glasses and he wore a tie to school every day. At recess, he'd always want to play radio with people and he'd run around with a tape recorder asking everyone to do interviews.

He had one friend, this kid Shane, who was like a math geek. Shane would play with Adam and stuff but he was a total chickensh_t when the other kids made fun of him. He never stuck up for him. I never made fun of Adam. I thought he was cute. He was one of those kids you just kind of knew would be famous one day. I was into celebrity mags like *OK!* and *Star* and *Tiger Beat*. They always had tons of stories about famous people who were bullied when they were in school too, like Christina Aguilera, Demi Lovato, even Adam

Levine, like OMG I know he's super old but he's still *totally* hot. He had acne when he was a kid and felt all awkward and stuff. The Adam at my school was sort of the same way, like, there was this whole other person inside of him that just hadn't been born yet. I felt bad that no one saw it but me.

Okay, so (sorry again, it *is* a bad habit, Mom's right, *arrrghhh!*). Anyway, this one day all these kids were picking on Adam really bad. They had his tape recorder and were playing catch with it. He was crying. They kept throwing it up in the air and then pretending like they were going to drop it. It was so mean. I went off on them. I told them to leave him alone, then I grabbed the tape recorder, gave it back to Adam, and told on them to the principal. I was never so mad. After that, all my friends turned on me. They said I was a tattletale. No one would talk to me. I stopped getting invited to sleepovers. No one would hang out with me or play with me at recess.

Then Adam won some radio contest for kids. It got in the papers and everything. All of the sudden, the other kids thought he was cool now. One day they hated him, and the next he was God. It was such BS. A group of kids who used to be my friends started messing with me at lunch. This one girl dumped juice all over my new white sweater on purpose. Adam was there. He saw it. She started laughing at me and then everybody else started laughing too. One kid said, "Hey, put some cold water on it, freak." Then he threw a whole bottle in my face. Adam was laughing at me with everybody else.

I hated them all. Now I just hate myself. I became just like them. Everybody treated Eric like crap. Why did I have to do it, too? I never even thought about it until today. Now I can't think about anything else. I hope being friends with Eric will help the old me, the one I liked, the one who stuck up for people, the one who was a good person, make the mean bitch who took over my body in middle school go away. I swear, I'll never be mean to anyone again. I swear I won't.

*Gemma, your story is a wake-up call to anyone who's a bully now who wasn't always that way. Sometimes when we get hurt really bad, it can make us angry and bitter, and the sweet part of us, the kind, compassionate, generous person inside, goes into hiding, and a bully takes over. What you proved is that just because that good person inside hasn't come out in a while, doesn't mean she isn't there. Eric truly was your hero because he helped you find the real Gemma again, the one who had the courage to speak up today, ask for forgiveness, and truly appreciate the forgiveness she was given. You've inspired a lot of people today, Gemma.*

*I also want to say something to Eric. Gemma's right. You ARE a hero. You're honest and compassionate, you have a heart the size of the sun, and you understand the power of forgiveness. Some people, when they've gone through a lot of pain and disappointment, hold grudges and they stay mad at the world. They become hostages of their own inability to forgive, and it not only holds them back, but it holds back whoever they're angry at, too. By forgiving Gemma and her friends, you allowed them to forgive themselves. That's a gift that only a real hero can give.*

*One last point I'd like to make is about Asperger's. If anyone listening now is struggling with Asperger's like Eric, it doesn't have to define you. Some kids have more severe cases of it than others, but it doesn't mean that you're broken or that you shouldn't have a full, rewarding life. Eric isn't broken; he's beautifully, wonderfully whole! There are support groups for kids with Asperger's and their families. There are doctors who specialize in treating Asperger's. Ask your parents to do their research and find these and other outlets where you can get information, help, and make friends with others who understand what you're going through. Concerning school, there are laws protecting kids with disabilities and special needs. Some school administrators and personnel don't know the laws, and others don't always enforce them. If there are parents listening in, if your child has Asperger's or is dealing with any type of social, physical, or learning challenge, know the laws. Know your rights. The more knowledge you have, the better it will be for everyone, including the school.*

*Gemma, thank you again for talking with us today and for introducing us to Eric. You both live in my heart and I know you've touched a lot of lives today.*

## CHAPTER FIFTEEN

# Gabe

I'm seriously into playing *Minecraft*. It's way better than other games. You have to be really smart to keep people from griefing you. Sorry, I do that a lot. I talk like everybody knows all that stuff. Griefing is when someone destroys what you built. Like in *Minecraft*, you get to build this awesome base. A base could be a house or a whole castle with all kinds of cool stuff. Anyway, it's kind of complicated but like if someone griefs you, that means they burn down your base or they can blow it up with TNT. They could even take it down piece by piece. It's radical. Most kids who are just getting into it don't know you have to claim your base to protect it, so they get messed with a lot. *Minecraft* is like the real world on super-steroids. It's cool once you know how it works.

I'm Gabe. Yo! I'm a freshman. I'm a gamer, like you couldn't tell already, LOL, but I'm not a geek or all dark and goth. I want to major in engineering in college, so when my parents get on my case about playing *Minecraft* too much, I tell them it's "honing my skills." I read that on Wikipedia. Dad still makes me get offline and do my homework.

My parents are pretty cool, except for that (only kidding, Dad). Dad's a commercial airline pilot. Mom sells real estate. They still act all mushy with each other. They go on dates together and sometimes they even kiss in public. Gross. Anyway, it's like they're still crushing on each other. I have a little brother, Joaquin. He's only five. Mom says he was our family's special surprise. Geez, Mom, like I don't know what a change-of-life baby is. I learned about it in health. It's like when a woman gets old and her period stops, and she thinks she can't get pregnant, and then she does. It's an "oops baby."

Hey, that's pretty funny, LOL. Did I tell you I'm like super funny? I make my parents laugh all the time, except the beginning of high school. It was the worst time of my life. High school wasn't what I expected. In fact, it sucked sh_t at first. People put a label on you—stoner, skater, brain, jock, whatever—and no one cares who you really are. I found that out quick.

I wasn't going to tell my story but everybody here was like, "None of us are gamers, we want someone who was bullied the way you were to talk about it." So here I am. I don't know if you're into *Minecraft* or not, or if you've ever played, but it's like totally awesome except when someone uses it to hate on you. Then it's no game. It's chickensh_t too because you can f___ with people in your character, so you can pretend like, "Hey dude, it wasn't me, it was just my character." It can get so messed up. I wonder if avatars can commit suicide, and if they do, does it mean the real person dies in a way too? It's heavy sh_t, man. A lot of kids are into AI—that stands for artificial intelligence, like robots and stuff, and computers that can think and feel, kind of like if that Siri chick on people's iPhones had a mind of her own. It's not all that whacked out. When you play these games, it's like your avatar is your reality. Seriously.

I could tell after eighth-grade graduation that my friends weren't into hanging out anymore. We hardly saw each other over the summer. The way our school district works didn't help either. It's so messed up. My three best friends are going to a different high school than me just because they live a few blocks past some BS border. It totally sucks. Only one of my friends is going to my high school, and he's got a girlfriend. He never hangs with anyone but her.

When I started high school I had to make all new friends. There was this one dude, Sly. He was pretty cool, totally into *Minecraft*. We got tight right away. He had a group of friends and they all played together. He asked me to join his group. I was psyched. These dudes were serious masters of the game. They knew sh_t even I wasn't hip to. They had all these cool profile names too, like DizzleHorse, Firehawk, and Cubinator. Mine was InfinityMaster. I picked that name because I wanted whatever I built to last forever, and I'm the master of my own destiny.

Oh yeah, I'm really into destiny and stuff. Like, my favorite play is this really cool ancient Greek tragedy called *Oedipus Rex*. My dad got me into it. It's this story about a dude named Oedipus. This psychic, actually, back then they called them oracles, told him he was going to kill his dad and marry his mom. He freaked out and tried to run away. He hit some guy in his carriage by accident, the guy died, and he ended up marrying his wife. Turned out, and this is *so* sick, they *were* his parents; he was adopted and she was his mother. Wild, right? OMG. The dude was so blown that he like poked his own eyes out. It was his fate.

Sorry, I drifted. Back to *Minecraft*. Yeah, so I wanted a profile name that said I was master of my fate, at least in the game, LOL. Sly set up a private server, and that's where we played. A lot of times we'd all Skype each other while we were playing. Everything was way cool until this huge drama at school. It's kind of a long story. Sly's grades started to go down. He was getting Ds and Fs. His parents were freaking, so they told him no more *Minecraft* or Internet until he got his grades back up. He was pissed. He started pulling some seriously stupid sh_t, like ditching class and smoking doobers under the bleachers at school. It was like he *wanted* to get in trouble. Sometimes he came to school drunk or high. The school counselor wasn't doing sh_t about it either. There were 800 kids in my grade and only two counselors for all of them. Most kids didn't even know who their counselor was. I never met mine. Like whatever.

Things with Sly got really f___ed up. One night he called me and said he was going to sneak out of the house, but he was grounded, and he wanted me to meet him. We live in one of those suburbs that's like a small town. You can walk to everything. Anyway, we met at Starbucks and Sly was all hyper and nervous. He said there was this cool party at some-one's house and we were going. I was like, "Whose house?" He goes, "Just some house, ya gotta chill, dude, okay?" In my head I was thinking, "No, this is definitely *not* okay," but I didn't want to be a pussy so I go, "Sure."

Big mistake. Let me say it again. Big mistake. It was weird but I didn't really know Sly that well. Our avatars knew each other from *Minecraft*, but the real people attached to the ava-tars didn't. I also never hung out with Sly and those guys in person. My whole social life was on computer. All this sh_t was running through my head walking to this party. I had a bad feeling.

We got to the house. It was nasty-looking, like seriously run down and stuff. I could hear old people's music like AC/DC playing. Sly knocked on the door. I was *so* not into it. This dude came out of the house. He had tattoos all over his arms and chest. He wasn't wearing a shirt. He high-fived Sly, then looked at me and said hi. I don't remember his name. He was a creep. I just wanted to get out of there, but like an idiot, I followed Sly and weird, scary dude into the living room. The whole place reeked of ganja and beer. There were a bunch of older kids there, all stoners. Sly's bud, "Weird Dude," handed Sly a beer and a joint. Sly took a toke. I wasn't into pot. I'd smoked it in eighth grade and all it did was make me hungry and tired. I didn't want anyone to think I was a wuss, so I took a toke too. It was harsh, made me hack up a lung. Yeah, fun. Anyway, so, then this lady came out of a back bedroom. She was wasted and slutty-looking. "Weird Dude" goes, "This is my mom." I wanted out of there so bad.

Then, Sly took me into the kitchen. There was some skinny-assed dude who smelled like sh_t smoking out of a bong. I go to Sly, "Look, dude, I'm outta here." Sly was already wasted. It's like he didn't even hear me. He gave me a pill and told me to swallow it. I go, "No way dude!" He goes, "Come on, it's X, you'll love it." So I go, "F___ off, asshole!" He wanted to hit me but he was too out of it. I ran outside and called my parents. I told them to pick Sly and me up. Stupid f___ing me.

I have to give my parents serious props for not freaking out when they got to the house. They were seriously cool. They told "Weird Dude" they were taking me and Sly home. My dad went into his pilot mode, like all stern and in charge, and I think he scared the sh_t out of "Weird Dude," because he just goes, "Hey, man, whatever." Sly was tripping. He was so out of it, he didn't know what the f___ was going on. My dad and I had to hold him on either side to get him into the car. When we got to his house, his parents were waiting outside by the porch. My parents had called them right after I called from the party. His mom was crying. I'd never met his parents before. They seemed like really nice people. They thanked me and my parents over and over, and his mom told me that Sly was lucky to have a true friend like me. Sly didn't feel that way. He hated me now.

Sly didn't come back to school for a month. His parents had to put him in rehab. His friends all blamed me. We were still playing *Minecraft*, but now it was them against me. Sly couldn't play 'cause there was no Internet at the rehab place. His friends started raiding my base all the time. Sorry, that means stealing sh_t from me. It's part of the game, but there's a difference between playing *Minecraft* 'cause it's fun and playing to seriously mess with someone's head. Then, my base got griefed, and when we'd Skype during games, they started threatening me. Things went really dark fast. I know it's just a game, but when you're into it, it's way more than that. Then one day after school by the bus stop, Sly's friends beat me up. I tried to hide it from my parents. I told them I fell in gym class. They looked at me like "Right, dude, we believe you, *not.*" They wanted to tell the principal but I freaked out. I told them it would only make things worse. That night, when I went on the server to play, I was banned. I should have expected it, but it's like the game was supposed to be separate, like it was one world, and real life at school was another. Every day, I took more sh_t. Being banned from *Minecraft* bothered me way more than getting messed with physically. It sounds pathetic, but if you're into gaming, you totally get it.

There were a few other groups of kids in my class who played, and I played with them a few times, but they pulled the same sh_t Sly's friends did. They let me get my base up and then they started f___ing with me, and then, I'd get banned. I played on a public server a couple of times too, but the noise was out about what I did at the party, and my name was in the sh_tter. Life sucked. I even bought a second profile and set it up, but the kids at school figured out it was me and the same thing happened.

My parents finally did go to the principal. By then, I didn't care. The principal said he'd talk to Sly's friends. He couldn't suspend them for beating me up after school because they all denied it and there were no witnesses; it was their word against mine. He did suspend them for threatening me on *Minecraft*. Their parents were pissed and said the principal couldn't punish their kids for something they did outside of school "in character" in a "fictional setting." The principal didn't see it that way. He said bullying was bullying and he was going to teach them and every other kid a lesson who used online gaming as a "weapon of cruelty." The whole thing became a big drama. At the school board meeting, there were tons of parents. Half of them agreed with the principal; the other half didn't. It was so weird 'cause parents were acting worse than their kids, screaming at each other and calling each other names. The principal didn't give in. He said if they wanted to get him fired, go ahead, but he wasn't going to back down on the gaming thing. I thought I'd have to go through school the most hated guy in my class, and then

Sly came back from rehab. He looked like a totally different dude. He looked healthy. He wasn't skinny and all strung-out anymore. He told me he was happy I called my parents that night and they picked us up. He said things were worse than I thought, that he was doing all kinds of drugs and f___ing up, and that I probably saved his life.

His friends wanted me to be a part of their *Minecraft* clique again, but I said no. Gaming is cool and I'll always do it but I finally figured out that I needed real friends to hang with and do stuff together in person. Skyping and gaming was like having a virtual social life. It was weird and I finally got the memo. It's like I was living my life through an avatar. I got lost and it took getting my ass kicked to see it.

It's second semester freshman year. Sly is my best friend. We still play *Minecraft*, but with other dudes now who are way cooler. And we do other dude stuff like hang out at the mall when we know the hot chicks from school will be there, play basketball at the rec center, you know, real life sh_t. My parents think I'm finally growing up. It's wild.

There's something I want to say before I bounce. If you're into gaming like I was, that's cool. I totally get it, but don't let it own your ass. Do other stuff too, hang out and chill with real live people. It's so easy to get lost in gaming, and it's not cool when your avatar is getting more action than you. I guess my dad's right when he says, "You've got to have balance." Balance is cool. Really, *really* cool.

*Gabe, your story is important. For those of you listening who are into gaming like Gabe, he's right. You can't let it own you. It can be a part of your social life, but it shouldn't represent all of it. If you know someone is using a game to bully or threaten someone else, speak up. Tell your principal or counselor at school. Bullying is wrong and cruel whether it's being done face to face or through an avatar.*

*I also want to comment on Gabe's integrity. That night at the party, he did the right thing calling his parents. It took real courage to not only protect himself but to watch out for Sly, too. Sometimes you may find yourself in a similar situation but you're afraid your friends will turn on you if you call for help. If they're your real friends they'll understand, if not at first, eventually. If they're not, you're better off finding out the truth before it's too late. Never leave a friend in a dangerous spot. You have what it takes to do the right thing. I believe in you. We all believe in you. Find your strength. We've got your back.*

# CHAPTER SIXTEEN

# Connor

Hi, it's great to meet you. I'm Connor. I just graduated high school. I'm starting college in the fall. I want to major in education, be a school a principal or something. I don't want anyone to go through what I did. My principal was a piece of sh_t. I want to be the kind of principal kids can trust and who won't judge them. My principal had to leave the school partly 'cause of me. The whole thing started when I came out. It feels good not to have to hide it anymore.

You know how Jodee talks about "elite leaders" and "elite tormentors"? I was an "elite leader" at my school. I was popular but I never excluded anyone or put other kids down. My friends and I were totally into sports. I was on the basketball team, and I played soccer too. My best friend was Windsor. I know, weird name, right? Everybody made fun of his name when he was little. It's some family thing. Windsor was on the basketball team with me. Our school had the hottest cheerleaders. Windsor was really into this one cheerleader, Mariah. She had long brown hair and huge tits. Windsor wasn't the deepest guy on the planet. They started dating senior year but he was crushing on her since forever. Her BFF, Sky, was into me. I liked Sky, but not that way. I faked it a long time. I'll get to that part of the story later. Anyway, Sky was cool. She had short red hair and was kind of a tomboy. I don't know what it was about our school, but all the cheerleaders were totally hot. A lot of us guys used to joke around about it.

School was okay. I got good grades, had a solid group of friends, and we hung out a lot. Besides Windsor and the girls, there was Jeff, also on the basketball team, Ray Jay (I know, cool name), who was on soccer with me, and then Luke. We were like a posse. We did everything together. Jeff and Luke didn't have girlfriends. They were more about spreading the love. Windsor and me pretty much stayed with Mariah and Sky. Ray Jay had a different girl every week.

Everybody at school looked up to us. Even the parents liked us. We weren't into drugs; we drank some beer when we had parties, but nothing major. Our parents were all friends and they came to our games and cheered us on. Windsor's dad was like embarrassing he was so into the games. He was cool though. Like I said, school was okay. Then, the sh_t hit the fan. What happened isn't some story in a book either. It was real life, and man, did it suck.

There was this LGBT group of kids at my school. You probably know what that is but don't look it up if you don't. I'll just tell you. It's Lesbian, Gay, Bisexual, Transgender. Everybody made fun of them. My friends and me didn't, but Ray Jay and Luke laughed at them behind their backs sometimes. I went along with it once in a while but it made me feel like sh_t. I was one of them. I just hadn't been honest with myself yet. Okay, so I guess now I should tell you that part.

I knew I was different in kindergarten. I swear, it's the craziest thing, but I remember my first crush, and it wasn't on a girl. It was on another boy in my class. His name was Clay. He was like this macho little kid. It's true. The dude liked rolling in the dirt and mud fighting. He'd do wheelies on his tricycle. One day he was playing on the swings and he fell. Most other kids would start crying. He brushed himself off, got back on the swings, and started swinging higher. He had this fearlessness about him that I thought was so cool. Five years old and I was in love. I didn't know it at the time, but that's what it was. Clay and I were buds. We played in the sandbox together. We hunted for fossils in the park (we didn't find any but we were convinced there was a T. rex buried near the monkey bars, LOL), we played Nerf ball, and we made fun of girls. We both thought they were yucky. I know, don't even go there, and yes it is funny. Clay's family moved to another state when we were in first grade. I cried when he left. My parents just thought I was sensitive. I was; I mean, I am. But that's not why I cried. I felt like a part of myself left with him. (Clay, if you're reading this, hope I haven't freaked you out.)

Some people think if you're gay you were born with it, that it's like the color of your eyes. Other people think it's how your parents raised you, like, maybe 'cause of some intense vibe from your mom, if she was all overprotective and mushy with you when you were growing up, it could make you gay. My mom was cool. She was the total opposite of overprotective. She let me get scrapes and fall down and stuff when I went outside to play. She'd say, "You have to eat a bucket of dirt before you die."

Dad was cool too. He and Mom worked together. They still do. Dad's an executive at a marketing company and Mom's his top salesperson. Yeah, they work together and live together and haven't killed each other yet. Like I said, my parents are cool. I love them. They've never pushed me like so many other parents do to their kids to be what they want them to be. They always told me to follow my own dreams.

That's why it was so hard for me to come out. Here I was, this popular dude at school, tons of friends, a drop-dead gorgeous girlfriend, and I was a good student, too. My parents were proud of me. It's not that I was afraid to tell them I was gay, or at least that I thought I was gay, 'cause I'd never even kissed anyone but Sky. It was more like if I told them, it would make it too real. I wasn't sure if I was ready for the truth to be that real in my own head.

I knew my parents would be okay with it. They wouldn't be thrilled. They'd do what they always did when I gave them bad news, like the time I flunked my math final. There wasn't any big mystery there. I was lazy and blew off studying. Anyway, when I told my parents, they didn't even tell me they were disappointed in me. Instead, they hugged me, told me they loved me, and that they were going to study with me every day until I got my math grade back up. "We'll conquer this challenge together," they said. I knew if I said I was gay, it would be the same thing. They might not like it, but they'd never turn their backs on me. They'd probably join some support group for parents of gay kids, learn as much about the gay lifestyle as they could, and start helping me adjust to the "challenges." I just wasn't ready to accept it about myself.

The LGBT kids at my school were my secret role models. They were so frickin' comfortable in their own skin. One of them, this guy Drake, was transgender. He hadn't had the surgery yet, but his aunt and uncle said after graduation, they would take him to doctors to see if it's something he really wanted. He did. He talked about it all the time at school, even wrote an extra-credit paper on it for science class. He lived with his aunt and uncle because his parents kicked him out of the house. That was after his dad beat the crap out of him for being a "f___ing sissy boy." I hated his parents. His mom was the sissy. She never even stuck up for him. She watched while her husband beat her son and never did jack. Sh__ty parents. Anyway, Drake always came to school dressed like a girl. He wore makeup and even sounded and acted like a girl. I guess I should really call him a she 'cause that's the way Drake thought of herself. She really was a girl on the inside. She wanted the surgery to make her a girl on the outside too. I got that. I respected her for it. Funny thing about Drake, she said when most transgender kids live as the sex they really feel they are, they have to change their names. She said the one good thing her parents did was give her a name that worked for a boy or a girl. She was happy she didn't have to change it.

There was this other kid in the LGBT group, Lola. She was a lesbian. I totally dug her, not like that way, but just as a person. She was really tough-looking. She had short hair, like a buzzcut, and wore guy T-shirts, jeans, and combat boots. She was like a guy, but still a chick. Her girlfriend was also in the group. Her name was Mallory. She was the opposite of Lola. Mallory was really feminine. There was still an edge about her that you didn't see in straight girls, but she was, I don't know how to put it, softer I guess. They really seemed to care about each other. They'd hold hands in the hallways and stuff. They kissed once by the lockers and got into big trouble. They were both suspended for two days. I thought that wasn't fair. Lots of kids kiss between classes. If they start making out, they might get a detention. Lola and Mallory got suspended 'cause they were both girls. I had a serious problem with that. But that was our school. Our principal was a holy-roller homophobe. He thought gays were sinners, and he was constantly trying to get the parents of the LGBT kids to send them to these weird Christian summer camps where they "cure you."

Some of the LGBT kids at school had okay parents. Others like Drake were stuck with parents who were ashamed of them. I was ashamed of *myself*, not for being gay, but for knowing it and being afraid to face it. I'd watch the LGBT kids at lunch. They sat together and even though they got made fun of, and people spit in their food or said really cruel sh_t to them, they knew who they were. They owned it and weren't scared to be themselves. I was always terrified if Windsor and my friends knew I was gay, they'd freak. I mean, *freak*. The one person I didn't think would be surprised was Sky. We'd been going out for two years, and we'd never done it. We kissed, I touched her down there a few times, she was totally into it, but then I'd stop. I'd tell her it was 'cause I respected her and didn't want to take advantage of her. Sky bought it in the beginning, but after a while, she started to wonder. Once she even asked me if I was gay. I didn't know what to say. She hugged me and said it was okay, I didn't have to answer, that she'd always love me, even if it was just as friends. Like I said, Sky was really cool. After that day, we'd kiss sometimes in the hall, but we both knew, it was so no one would figure out the truth until I was ready. I've never admitted this to anyone, but sometimes when I'd be kissing Sky, I'd pretend it was a guy I'd seen on TV or at school that I liked.

It got to be really hard living a lie. It made me feel like no matter how much I showered, I wasn't clean.

Then, something happened and it's not like I came out; it's more like I got pushed out. Drake tried to kill herself. Her aunt found her in the garage in her cousin's car with the motor on and the garage door down. She would have died too but I guess God put His foot down. Drake had timed it so her aunt would be at work when she did it. The aunt forgot some papers she needed and had to turn around and go back to the house.

Drake had to stay in the hospital for a week for "evaluation." I found out that the reason she tried to commit suicide was because the principal told her she had to start dressing and acting like a boy or she was getting kicked out of school. Her aunt and uncle were fighting it, her parents were taking the principal's side, the whole thing was a f___ed-up mess, and Drake was in the middle. I went to visit her in the hospital. Drake said she went to the principal about starting an LGBT club at the school, and the principal freaked, said no way was he going to support any clubs for fags and perverts. Drake said the principal called her horrible names and told her she'd burn in hell. I told Drake she should have taped the conversation on her phone. Drake said her aunt and uncle were going to fight the school.

Drake was lucky her aunt and uncle were on her side. Her parents and the principal were so wrong. I finally decided it was time for me to be honest with myself and everyone else. I was scared sh_tless. For two days I didn't eat or sleep. I came clean with Windsor, Ray Jay, Jeff, Luke, and Mariah. I told them I was gay. Everyone took it good, except Windsor. We'd bunked together at summer camp, shared rooms together for out-of-state games. He was like, "All that time you were looking at me like *that*, man?" I tried to explain that just because someone is gay doesn't mean they crush on every person of the same sex. I was like, "Do you like every single girl?" He said, "No, but that's different." I was like, no it's not. I said to him, "Hey man, you're not my type anyway." I was trying to lighten things up, plus he really wasn't my type. He didn't think it was funny. In that moment, I knew we would never be friends again. It was like he shut the door in my face. He just couldn't handle a gay best friend.

The rest of the gang, even though they acted okay with it, didn't want me hanging with them anymore. I was sad for a while; then I realized, I could either be a victim and feel sorry for myself or use the pain like gas in a car.

I talked to my parents about it. Oh yeah, I came out to them that night, after I told my friends. They said they always knew. Can you believe that sh_t? Mom said there were so many times she wanted to ask me about it and let me know she and Dad loved me no matter what, but they decided to wait until I was ready to open up. It was such a relief. They knew about what happened to Drake. I told them I wanted to help Drake start an LGBT club at the school and that the first step was taking on the principal. Even though I only had half a year left of high school, I wanted Drake and me to make a difference that would be remembered. They were in. They contacted the parents of the other LGBT students and started a parents group. A few didn't want anything to do with it, but most, like Drake's aunt and uncle, were psyched to get involved. That was the beginning. I won't go into all the details 'cause it would take like forever, but the parents group and all the kids prepared a presentation for the school board meeting. It turned out it wasn't just Drake who the principal had called names and humiliated. He'd done it to lots of other people too. One of them had it recorded on his phone. He played the recording at the school board meeting. The principal stood up like he was going to say something, but somebody's dad forced him to sit back down and be quiet. Some of the school board members looked like they were going to be sick. One woman kept staring at the principal, shaking her head.

Our superintendent wasn't a strong guy. Confrontation freaked him out. He made the principal take an "early retirement," and he gave us the okay for a club. He told us we had to be "respectful and appropriate," and no "public displays of affection." He made that rule for everybody though, no more kissing in between periods. Mariah and Windsor were pissed. They were always sucking face. Whatever.

Drake finally came back to school. She and I were the leaders of the club. For the first time in my life I felt comfortable in my own skin. I felt real and true and alive and honest. I won't say life was perfect my last semester senior year. A lot of the guys on basketball and soccer gave me sh_t. I ended up having to quit the teams. That was really rough. I loved sports and it was like something important was stolen from me. One of my teachers told us that "High school is a microcosm for the real world." That means it's like a mini-version of life that's supposed to help prepare you for sh_t. It did. I'm totally ready for college.

If you're gay or transgender, and you're afraid to come out, please listen to me: living a lie isn't worth it. It sounds corny but the truth really will set you free. It did for me. I know you might feel kind of alone right now, but you're not. You've got all of us and we are standing right here beside you. You have real courage. We can see it inside of you. It's time for you to see it too.

*Connor, you've helped a lot of kids today. Thank you for talking with us. I'd like to point out a couple of things. First, your principal was so wrong to treat LGBT students as he did. Some principals are wonderful and supportive and others like Connor's are closed-minded and unkind. If anyone listening now is dealing with a similar situation as Connor or Drake, it's important you know that no one should discriminate against you for your sexual orientation or gender. No one—that means other students, teachers, administrators, bosses, no one. If you're being discriminated against or made to feel as if there's something wrong with you that needs to be "cured," don't allow the abuse to continue. Speak up! Tell an adult you trust and ask for support and help. Whether that adult is one of your parents, the parent of a friend, a teacher or mentor, look him in the eye, be honest, and explain what's going on. There are also websites and support groups for LGBT teens. Do some research online and see what's available in your community. Make an effort to meet other LGBT teens and build meaningful friendships. Connor's right. You're not alone. We are here and we know you can get through this.*

*Lastly, be proud of who you are. There's no shame in being different. The only shame is in hiding it. You are perfect the way you are. You have your whole life ahead of you. Start living it now in truth and confidence!*

# CHAPTER SEVENTEEN

# Savannah

I'm Savannah, but everyone calls me Savvy. Hi. It's good to meet y'all. I'm a junior. The kids at my school are rich. A lot of them are sort of stuck-up too. It's a college prep academy. Almost everyone at this school has been going here since kindergarten, and they all are from wealthy families. I'm not. My family didn't have anything until my dad inherited a bunch of money from some uncle he never knew he had. Turns out my granddad had a brother who didn't want to be a sh_tkicker his whole life, so he ran away, never came back. My granddad never mentioned him. My dad thought it was a joke until some lawyer from New York showed him the paperwork and it was legit. I guess my dad was his only living heir. The whole thing was crazy.

We inherited a lot. We went from poor to rich overnight. That's when my parents transferred me out of public school to the academy. I didn't start here until sophomore year. That's why I'm not stuck-up. When I was little, we lived in a trailer and people thought we were white trash. I was never trash, but try telling anyone in our town that.

I'm hoping that y'all won't judge me when you hear my story. I'm embarrassed and ashamed about what happened. I made a giant fool of myself 'cause of my boyfriend. He was fixin' to dump me anyway. I wish I could get me a time machine and go back to that day. I'd 'a never done it. I'd 'a told him to go straight to hell. Instead, I went along with him 'cause I loved him crazy and I was afraid I'd lose him if I didn't. My parents are scared it'll make it harder for me to get into a good college now. I guess I'm worried about that too, but mostly I'm just happy to be able to walk down the street again without being stared at or having people whisper behind my back about what a "slut" I am. They still gossip about it, but it's died down some.

I'm not a slut, but I'm jumping ahead. I do that sometimes when I get nervous. Sorry y'all. Anyway, so, I pretty much got along with everyone at school but sometimes I know they looked down on me. I was raised so different than the other kids. I wanted them to like me. I tried to keep up with how the popular girls dressed and did their makeup. I pretended to like the same TV shows and music. I even tried out for gymnastics 'cause someone said all the hot girls were on the team. I made the team and it turns out I'm really good at the parallel bars. You should see the trophies I won. My mom has them on a shelf in my bedroom. This would have been my third year in gymnastics. I got kicked off. It was awful.

Anyways, before that, I made myself fit in at school. It was like an extra-credit project that never ended. I had to constantly keep working on it. Sometimes I wanted to be the old public school me again, the one who was into Charlie Daniels, Johnny Cash, and Willie Nelson. I wanted to wear real cutoff jeans and not those fancy True Religion kind, and eat chicken-fried steak, not all that tofu stuff. Instead, I acted like I was into everything the academy kids were. I listened to Taylor Swift and Rascal Flatts even though I'd rather be hearing anything else. I wore designer jeans that were so expensive I was scared to get them dirty, and dressing up meant lululemon yoga pants with UGG boots. I hate UGG boots.

I know what you're thinking. You're probably saying to yourself, Savvy was a phony. In some ways, I was, but I wasn't fake in my heart. I cared about my friends and I worked hard at my grades, and I didn't lie. Well, maybe I sorta lied, but I didn't cheat or steal. I never made fun of people the way a lot of other kids did, and I stuck up for the underdog too.

The person I lied to worst was me. I was so in love with my boyfriend, Trace, that I'd do anything for him and I convinced myself he loved me too. He was just so beautiful. I know that seems like a weird word to describe a guy, but he really was beautiful. It wasn't just how he looked. Yeah, his body was to die for and he had the sexiest smile you ever saw, but his personality made me melt whenever he was around. When Trace walked into a room, he owned it. He made everybody feel important, even the people no one paid attention to.

I remember once we were at the grocery store getting some snacks. Somebody had spilled a bottle of ketchup and this poor janitor was on his hands and knees cleaning it up. He was older and looked tired and sad. Trace just started talking to him like he'd known the guy forever. He made him feel special; you could see it in his face. No one ever took the time to even say hello to him, but Trace asked him about his job, what he liked to do in his time off, like they were old friends. That was Trace. He just knew how to make people feel good about themselves. Trace was like a rock star. He used to yell, "Woo hoo!" when he was happy about something, and he'd get a big smile on his face and start running around saying it, "Woo hoo! Woo hoo!" He was like a little kid. Trace made everyone around him feel good. I was so in love with him, I used to stare at him like I was looking at a painting, and each time, I saw something new and beautiful that I hadn't seen before.

Being Trace's girlfriend wasn't always easy though. He could be a handful. His dad was a big real estate developer. Trace was used to getting what he wanted when he wanted it. He wasn't a jerk or anything but sometimes he could be a spoiled brat.

We'd make out in this old barn near his parents' house, and we almost went all the way a couple of times but I wasn't ready. I was still a virgin. By the beginning of junior year, all the other girls in my class had gone all the way. My best friend, Ally, had already had sex with four boys, and she says the first one didn't even count 'cause he wore a condom. I said to her, "What does that matter, y'all still *did it*," but she was like, "Nope, didn't count." I know, crazy. Like I said, I was raised so different. My other best friend, Becca, lost her virginity over the summer. I did give Trace a BJ once, thinking that would tide him over. It might've too, if his stupid friends weren't on his case every dumb minute.

Trace wasn't a virgin. He'd been doing it since middle school. That's why his friends were giving him sh_t. They kept asking him if there was something wrong with me, if I had some disease or something. They were really mean about it. I could tell they were starting to get to Trace, especially Bo. He was Trace's best friend since kindergarten.

I never liked Bo. He was too damn big for his britches. His family owned an old hotel. It was on one of those snooty lists of "national landmarks." People came from all over to stay there. A few miles away there was a big outdoor concert place where lots of bands played. The stars always stayed at Bo's family's hotel. Bo was always bragging about the famous people he hung out with. My parents said Bo acted like a showoff 'cause he was insecure. My mom and dad knew Bo's parents pretty well. Everybody knows everybody in our town and no one ever minds their own business.

I don't know if you've ever been in love, but it can really suck. Trace made me believe I could trust him. He was so good to me, and when we were together, he gave me all his attention. My girlfriends were always so jealous 'cause their boyfriends weren't like that. They'd break dates all the time and they were never romantic like Trace. Trace was the most romantic guy on earth. Like, we'd be hanging out with a bunch of our friends, and he'd be sitting across from me, and I'd get a text that'd say, "I can't wait for us to be alone." I loved those texts. They made me feel so sexy and special.

There were some hot springs near my house. Sometimes, Trace and I would sneak in at night, and he'd bring a washcloth and bathe me in the springs. He'd wash my face and my chest, and kiss my back. He told me he'd wait for me forever, that he respected me for being a "good girl." He told me I could tell him anything, that I could trust him with my life. He'd e-mail me love songs. He sent me this one song about if he ruled the world, I'd be his queen, and he'd protect me. My favorite was when he e-mailed me a video of Adele singing "Love Song." I remember this one part of the lyrics, "However long I stay, I will always love you, whatever words I say, I will always love you." This little voice in the back of my head said, it was like a warning, that even though he'll always love me, he wouldn't stay. Every second we spent together after that, I held on tight, breathing in every detail of every second, so it would stay with me forever.

The night it happened was so weird. I was home alone. My parents were at a movie. Trace texted me to send him a sexy selfie. He'd never done that before. I was like, "Seriously?" He texted, "Yeah, send me one of you in your bra." I felt really uncomfortable but I was scared I was losing him. Between the Adele video and Bo always putting me down to him, I figured it wasn't that big of a deal. I asked him if he was alone. He texted back, yes. I said, do you promise you won't show it to anyone and that you'll delete it right away? He said, yes. I asked him again to promise me. He said, yes, he promised. So I took off my T-shirt, took a selfie, and texted it.

"That's good, baby," he texted back. "But why don't you take out one of your breasts and let me see some real skin?" I was like, you see my breasts in person, why do you need a picture, but he texted it was sexier this way, and more fun. I said no, but he kept pushing. "Come on, don't be a chicken," he said. So I did it. Then, he wanted a selfie of me naked. I told him no way, but he said no one else would see it and he promised me, *promised* me he would delete it. I felt so uncomfortable, but I wanted to make him happy. I locked my bedroom door, got undressed, laid on my back naked in bed, and took a picture. I looked thin and curvy 'cause of the angle of my phone camera. I texted Trace the picture. He asked me for another and then another, with different poses. I know something should have stopped me but he acted so, I don't know, what's the word here, *grateful*.

Finally, I told him no more, and to delete every single picture. He texted me thank you like a gazillion times, and that he loved me and would see me tomorrow at school.

I never made it to school the next morning, or the morning after that, or the one after that. I couldn't leave the house for a month. If it wasn't for my teachers sending home my assignments, I would've had to do my whole junior year over. Trace wasn't alone when I texted him those photos. Bo was there with two of his other friends. The whole thing was a dare. Trace didn't want to look like a pussy so he went along with it. Bo forwarded the texts to all their other friends. He and Trace should have gotten expelled but their parents gave so much money to the school—the library was named after Bo's great-granddad—that the school just swept everything under the rug, pretended like it never happened. The headmaster "suggested" to my parents that they keep me home for a while. He said to wait until it blew over.

My parents were mega disappointed in me, but they were more upset with Trace. My mom and dad loved him like a son. They couldn't believe he could be that mean and weak. Trace's parents blamed me, told my parents that if I wasn't such a slut in the first place, I would have told their son to go "jump in a lake," that it was up to the girl to stop "that sort of thing," and that Trace was just being "playful," 'cause "you know how boys will be boys."

When I finally did go back to school, I just wanted God to give me cancer. Ally and Becca wouldn't talk to me. They wouldn't even look at me. Someone wrote "slut" all over my locker in black marker, and I found porn magazines in my backpack with a note, "Why don't you send them some pictures, bitch!" Nowhere was safe. A bunch of girls cornered me in the locker room after gym, threw me onto the floor, and dumped yogurt all over me. I had to go to the nurse's office and wait for my mom to bring me a change of clothes.

I could have gone home but I wanted to stick it out. I was doing okay until I saw Trace kissing this girl in the hall. He seemed so into her. It felt like a knife inside me. I just stood there paralyzed. He saw me watching them kiss, and he gave me this weird look, that said, like, "I'm sorry but it is what it is." I ran outside, hid under the bleachers, and sobbed. I was almost choking I was so upset. I still loved Trace; even after everything he did, I still loved him. Now I had no friends, no Trace, and everyone thought I was a slut. I asked God to give me cancer again.

Then, something happened inside me. I got mad. I thought, this isn't me. I'm better than this; I'm stronger than this. I called my mom and asked her to pick me up. Then that night, I wrote a letter to the editor of the local town paper. I told the story of what happened. I said I knew I was wrong, and I wanted to share my story so other kids wouldn't make the same mistake. At the end of the letter, and I can't believe I did this, I called out the headmaster of my school and the whole stinking board of trustees. I said we all should have at least gotten suspensions, that even though Trace and Bo were more at fault, I still didn't have to take the pictures or send them. The school should have done the right thing, taught us a lesson, made a statement, something, anything, but instead they did what they always did: hide the truth to "keep the peace." Well I wasn't feeling very "peaceful" and I said the academy was one of the oldest and most respected schools in the country, and it should set the standard for other schools, not skirt it. I ended the letter by saying that my parents and I were holding an open meeting about sexting and self-respect. I said in my letter that I hoped the headmaster and board of trustees would support our efforts, that we had a chance to make a difference and that they should be there.

The meeting wasn't packed, but it wasn't empty either. The headmaster was sitting in the front row looking nervous. I got up and spoke. My mom and dad spoke, and we had an expert from the phone company give a presentation about how once you text or post something on your phone, it stays around forever. You can't just get rid of it by deleting it. I saw some parents' faces as he was talking and you could tell he was scaring the sh_t out of them. It was a good thing. They needed to be scared. Like I said earlier, I'm hoping my story will scare all of y'all too from doing what I did.

It's the middle of junior year now. Things aren't perfect. I still miss Trace but I'm getting over it slowly. I'm seeing a therapist to help me understand myself better and become stronger as a person. The kids at school aren't messing with me anymore. The headmaster took care of that after the meeting. I'm really lonely, and I'm trying to make new friends outside of school. Mom and Dad found this really cool gymnastics club a few towns north, and I've been going four days a week. We have a competition next month and I can't wait. I've also started looking at colleges. My parents said if any of them somehow find out what happened, I should just tell the truth, let them know I went from being a victim to a survivor and a leader, and that they should want me in their school. I know senior year is going to be hard. I'm ready for it. I'm not the same girl I was six months ago. I like this new one much better.

*Savvy, I am blown away by your dignity and strength. You have such courage. I know what you went through was devastating. I've had my heart broken too by someone who had a personality a lot like Trace's. He was the most charismatic guy I never met. I still miss him sometimes. One of my favorite books, called* Broken Open, *is about how when something awful happens and your heart gets broken, it's in those moments that we have an opportunity to grow and evolve the most. Not everyone uses those opportunities. Some people let heartbreak and disappointment take the wind out of them and they never fully recover. You, Savvy, are an inspiration not just to me but to everyone who's listening here today.*

*I'd like briefly to discuss the whole texting/sexting thing. Savvy, I think you've already covered it so well, there's not much I need to add, except to emphasize to everyone listening right now that once any of you post something online or text it through your phones, it's forever. You can never take it back. Whatever you post lives on in infinity. So be careful. Think before you post. Think before you text. You are precious and beautiful, and don't let anyone force you into doing anything that could cause harm to yourself or others. Be strong. Stay alert. Most of all, remember your worth.*

*If any of you ever feels tempted to do something you know could hurt you, send me an e-mail for moral support. You're not in this by yourself. You have all of us. And we're here for you now and always.*

# Afterword

Almost any author will tell you that there is no feeling quite as exhilarating or bittersweet as typing "The end." Our books are like our babies. We give birth to them, nourish and protect them, and help them grow, until one day we must let go and set them free. A couple of days before I completed the manuscript for this book, I had to walk away from it for a day (writers hate to do that—most of us, when we're immersed in a book project, can't stand the thought of leaving our writing, not even for a second, let alone a whole entire day when we know our editor is waiting and deadlines must be met). It was a keynote for a major educational conference, and I had committed to it long before I conceived this book.

The flipside of being a writer is that when you've locked yourself away for months crunching on a book, it can be hard to get back into the groove. I'm also a speaker, and I give hundreds of talks a year. Going from writing to speaking mode, then back into the writing head isn't always easy. As soon as I finished the keynote, I was eager to return to my writing studio because I still had Chapter 17 to do, plus this Afterword, and I didn't want my editor getting nervous.

Making matters worse, I had no idea what I was going to talk about in the Afterword. Each time I thought about it, I drew a blank, the proverbial "writer's block." I'd done everything to get the creative juices flowing . . . yoga, running, meditation, and of course grilled cheese sandwiches with potato chips, a naughty treat for a health and fitness nut, but desperate times call for desperate measures. Nothing was working.

When I drove downtown for the keynote, I was a nervous wreck, wondering how on earth I was going to move and inspire fifteen hundred people, pull a ten-page chapter out of the air, and another ten-page Afterword all in the next seventy-two hours.

The organization that brought me in to speak had also requested two workshops and a book-signing session in addition to the keynote. I was grateful for the opportunity and of course said yes, not knowing that a year later I'd be sweating bullets on the deadline from hell the day of the event.

"Yep," I said to myself, "time to pray for a miracle."

They say that God works in mysterious ways. He does indeed, and He has a sense of humor, too. As I was finishing up my last workshop, several attendees approached me, commenting on how deeply I seemed to "get kids," the way they think and how they experience the world. I explained that as a survivor of bullying myself, having been the school outcast from fifth grade through high school, I knew firsthand the pain and loneliness, I understood the frustration, and that the secret to helping any child in crisis is being able to think in "kid head," and not "grownup head." Then I offered some tips on how to achieve this dramatic but necessary shift in perspective. It was then, as the group I was chatting with began to disperse, that two women came up to me. They were full of energy and personality, seeming bigger than life. One was a school psychologist, the other the director of a troubled youth program, the largest of its kind in her state. They were so effervescent and fun, I couldn't help but feel invigorated. They asked me if I had any new books coming out.

I know I should have been racing back to my computer and Chapter 17. I could almost feel my editor checking his e-mail but I just couldn't help myself. These two women were like sunshine, so I said, "Oh, yes," and I started telling them about this book. Before I knew it, an hour had gone by, most of the people at the conference had already left, and here we were still yacking away. (Did I mention there were multiple tornado warnings in the area, sirens were going off, cell phones were beeping, and outside the window, the sky was a sickly black and green hue like the color of a nasty bruise?)

Authors usually love to talk about their work—in fact, we can be downright bores sometimes—but when there are winds whipping against the building and the electricity is cutting on and off, you'd think that would at least merit a pause in the conversation.

You'd *think* that, yes, but this was no ordinary conversation. These two women, without even knowing it, gave me the inspiration for this afterword. It was funny, too, because as if in a flash of light, I knew exactly what I wanted to say. The words started coming so fast and furious that as we were still talking, I pulled up the notes app on my phone and started jotting down key points. In that moment—and here's the part where you can really see God's sense of humor—skies cleared, the winds died down, and the sun came peeking out. And . . . wait for it . . . a rainbow appeared!

I'm a huge *Wizard of Oz* fan, and Judy Garland has a special place in my heart. When I was little, I thought Dorothy was my guardian angel. To this day, whenever there's a rainbow, I feel hugged by the heavens.

To the two women I was talking with, if you're reading this now, you'll know who you are. Thank you for being such wonderful muses. The kids you work with are blessed to have you in their lives . . . and I was blessed to have met the kids in this book.

How I got to know these kids is amazing. The first book I wrote about school bullying, which started me on this adventure, was my memoir. Titled *Please Stop Laughing at Me . . .*, it chronicled my years as a bullied student. The moment it was published, kids from all over the country starting e-mailing me, crying for help. Most of them wanted me to come to their schools and speak. That was the genesis of what has now become my day-long, in-school anti-bullying program *It's NOT Just Joking Around!*™ When I go into a school to speak, I'll do student presentations, a teacher workshop, and a seminar for parents in the evening. The student presentations are dramatic. The middle-school and high-school talks are ninety minutes, during which I relive key scenes from my youth, and it's held together by a message-infused narrative.

My message has three parts:

1. Bullying isn't just joking around; it can damage you for life.

2. Bullying isn't just the mean things you do; it's all the nice things you never do.

3. If you are excluded or bullied, there is nothing wrong with you. It's often what's right about someone that makes them a target of cruelty.

After each student presentation, dozens of kids come up to me in tears. Most of them are victims of bullying, some of whom require a full-on intervention, of which I've done many. The rest, surprisingly, are bullies. Some are the mean popular students who I call "elite tormentors"; others are more traditional bullies. All of them have one aspect in common when they approach me—until they heard my presentation they never realized their behavior was mean, and they want me to help them make amends to the people they've hurt. I've participated in hundreds of interventions and worked with kids from every walk of life. Some stay in touch with me after I leave their school; other encounters are just the day I'm there. One thing is for sure: Each of these children has touched my soul in ways neither I nor probably they ever imagined.

In each case, I always ask them two questions—what have your parents and teachers done that helped, and what have they done that made things worse? The answers have always astounded me but not for the reason you may think. When I was a kid, there were certain things the adults in my life tried that did help, and other things that made me want to scream. I never forgot that list. The answers these kids give exactly mirror my own list. We have the same complaints about adults when it comes to handling bullying. These patterns aren't haphazard either. They're consistent from interview to interview—and I conduct literally thousands of interviews. There is little to no variation.

To me, these interviews prove that the world may change, but life and the adolescent heart remain the same. What bothered kids thirty years ago about grown-up behavior still bothers them now. As adults we can wax intellectual all we want about the Internet, progress, video games, the state of the country . . . we could go on and on.

The bottom line is that even without social networking, violence on television, cell phones, and all the other accoutrements of our modern age, kids are still kids. They hunger for the same thing: acceptance. When they're denied this vital emotional nutrient, they become sick inside. Most adults don't remember this sickness; after all, they're grown-up. Too often we trivialize it as drama.

It's not. Make no mistake. To a kid, fitting in is life or death. It's why so many young people take their own lives.

All of these things are why I wrote this book. In my previous books, I was always the one speaking to my young readers. Now it's time for them to hear from someone other than me, people who can reach them on a whole other level. Kids share a raw honesty and openness with each other that adults don't. That's why I wanted to give the kids a voice here. I needed *them* to be the storytellers.

There's nothing quite like hearing from a peer that you're going to be okay, that this awful period in your life will end, that things will get better, and that you can survive and reclaim your dignity. I can tell you this over and over, but while it might offer some inspiration, there is no substitute for a peer grabbing hold of your hand and walking you through a rough time. Kids look up to other kids more than they do adults. They share a secret world. I needed this book to reflect that world, the inner sanctum of adolescent truth, the real light at the end of the tunnel.

Listening to these stories and thinking about this, I found that nothing makes me angrier than hearing kids say that someone told them to just ignore the bullies and walk away. That's absolutely wrong. As the kids in this book have shown, you can fight back and you can win.

You can survive. We did.

# A Letter to Parents

I work with parents every day. They come to me struggling to understand where their child is coming from, wanting to know how to reach their son or daughter, how to help them. Some are parents of bullies; others are parents of victims or bystanders. I could fill an entire book with stories of moms and dads I've met who, despite the best intentions in the world, managed to make things worse for their child instead of better. It was always heartbreaking for me to see the agony on their faces, knowing they loved their kids, but their love was either too much, not enough, or sometimes, a little of both.

When I was being bullied, there were certain things my parents did that helped and certain things that made my life infinitely harder. Here's what I can tell you that I wish someone would have told my mom and dad all those years ago.

The old clichés like ignore the bully and walk away, they're just jealous, one day you'll look back on this and laugh, or I know how you feel—these don't work. They've never worked. Kids are smart. They know an empty cliché when they hear it and it only makes them feel more helpless. As adults, our instinct is to fix our kids' problems, but sometimes, what our children need isn't for their problem to be fixed. They just need someone to listen without judging them or (and here's a biggie) interrupting them. Too often, adults tend to interrupt kids and start offering advice before they even finish what they are trying to say. Then, when the kid becomes impatient over having been interrupted, the adult will chastise the child. It's always struck me as odd that adults do this. My advice to you: Listen to your child. Really listen. Don't offer advice unless your child asks for it. Adolescents can be very good at figuring out a solution to a dilemma on their own. Often they don't need an adult to tell them what to do; rather, they want someone to listen and provide a sounding board, someone with whom they can explore options and determine a logical plan of action.

Parents, I also want to stress the importance of compassion for the bully. I know, I know, that's a tricky one. I get it, believe me. As a former victim of bullies, I didn't always feel compassionate either. Here's the reality though. Most bullies are not mean because they have malice or hatred toward your child, but because they're going through something painful in their own lives and acting out. The more curious you are about the bully's backstory, the more you'll find out, and the more you know, the more compassion you're likely to feel.

Curiosity leads to compassion. Be curious. Find out as much about the bullies as you can. When you approach school administration, do so from a productive standpoint. Tell the principal you want to help *all* the kids involved, including the bullies, that you want *all* the kids to get the help and support they need. The school will view you with more respect because you're acting reasonably. You'll set a powerful example for your child about the importance of forgiveness and compassion. Most importantly, you'll have helped to neutralize a situation that, should it escalate, can only bring more pain to everyone.

Last, and I can't say this enough, don't live vicariously through your child. Perhaps you were bullied or excluded when you were in school and the wounds still affect you. Make sure, double-sure, that if your child is being bullied, you don't overreact because you're superimposing your own unresolved experiences onto your child's situation. Keep your past separate. If necessary, talk to a therapist. Most of the "helicopter" parents about whom administrators complain are the ones who haven't come to grips with their own teen years and seek to achieve this by fixing everything in their kids' lives. You need to have boundaries. Your past is your past. Your child's present is your child's. Keep it straight and if you can't, find a professional who can help you.

Thank you for loving your children. I know parenthood can be difficult. I know there are days when you feel as if you can't take one more minute of watching your son or daughter being hurt. Be strong. Hang in there. You're not alone. I'm here to help. Reach out to me via e-mail. I also have lots of parenting tips relevant to bullying in the survivor section of my website. I know how much you love your child. I can feel it as I'm writing this. There's no such thing as a perfect parent. Be present, listen, keep your heart and mind open, and always, always be honest with your child, no matter what.

Love and hugs,

Jodee Blanco

# Acknowledgments

I'm so grateful to so many people, I don't even know where to begin. As Glinda the Good Witch of the North said to Dorothy, "It's always best to start at the beginning."

This book would not be possible without the following people:

My editor at Adams Media and friend Peter Archer, who helped me grow as a writer in ways I didn't think possible. You are the most patient person on the planet . . . thank you for putting up with my insecure moments and helping me blossom. I am so blessed to have you in my life.

My friend Kent Carroll, who taught me how to write and what friendship truly is. I love you with all my heart.

My publisher Karen Cooper, Chris Duffy, Beth Gissinger, Lauren Rouleau, and all the other wonderful folks at Adams Media/F+W. Every author should work with a publisher like you. What a gift you all are. Thank you.

David Nussbaum, my publisher, friend, and an inspiration always. F+W is blessed to have you at its helm.

The members of Styx—James "JY" Young, Tommy Shaw, Chuck Panozzo, Lawrence Gowan, Todd Sucherman, and

Ricky Phillips. If it weren't for you guys lifting my tired spirits at this summer's opening concert, and the wonderful energy and friendship backstage, I would never have met my deadline for this book. Thank you for always being so kind and gracious to me over the years. And a special thank-you to JY for your support and encouragement.

My personal trainers, Margie Sefcik and Doris Kane, who kept me sane and healthy during the writing of this book. Thank you.

Debbie, Jessica, Gina, Rich, Jose, Daniel, and everyone at the Regency of Palm Beach, who put up with my craziness during the writing of this book. Thank you for understanding why an author needs quiet and always doing your best to provide it despite it being construction season. You are all saints!

Ben Schuh and his lovely mother, Elizabeth, who gave me a brilliant crash course on gaming—your help was priceless.

My girlfriends Becky Heim, Candace Kent, Maggie Sokolowski-McCarthy, Marilyn Kelly, and Margaret Sinnot, who made sure I took breaks and ate, and had a glass of wine every now and then during the writing of this book. Thank you for keeping me on track.

My beloved pets Ms. Roxy (who's in heaven now—I miss and love you) and Mr. Shadow, who remind me every day what unconditional love looks like.

My friend and colleague Bob Zmuda, who made me laugh on the hard writing days so I could get through another chapter. This book would never have gotten finished without you. Please thank Tony Clifton for me, too.

My mom and Donald "Deet" Taylor, who loved me through each and every chapter. I love you both, so much.

Lastly, I wish to thank every teen in this book and all the kids I've met and worked with touring America's schools. Each of you has touched my heart and given me courage. Without you, this book, and my life's purpose, wouldn't exist. I love you all.

# Index

## About the Author

Survivor, expert, and activist Jodee Blanco is one of the country's preeminent voices on the subject of school bullying. She is the author of the *New York Times* bestseller *Please Stop Laughing at Me . . . One Woman's Inspirational Story.* A chronicle of her years as a student outcast, the book inspired a movement inside the nation's schools and has become an American classic. Referred to by many as "the anti-bullying bible," it is required reading in hundreds of middle and high schools and many universities throughout the country. *Please Stop Laughing at Me . . .* has also been recognized as an essential resource by the National Crime Prevention Council, the Department of Health and Human Services, the National Association of Youth Courts, Special Olympics, the Family, Career and Community Leaders of America, the American School Counselor Association, *Teacher* magazine, and hundreds of state and local organizations from the PTA and regional law enforcement coalitions to school safety groups.

Blanco's award-winning sequel, *Please Stop Laughing at Us . . .* (BenBella Books), was written in response to the demand for more information from her core audience—teens, teachers, parents, and other adult survivors of peer abuse like herself. It provides advice and solutions set against the backdrop of her dramatic personal and professional journey. Blanco also released a companion journal to *Please Stop Laughing at Me . . .* entitled *The Please Stop Laughing at Me . . . Journal: A Safe Place for Us to Talk*, in which she helps draw teens out of silence to a place of renewed self-understanding and acceptance.

Blanco's unprecedented approach to shifting the social dynamic of America's schools is saving lives and making headlines throughout the United States. She has presented *It's NOT Just Joking Around!*, her acclaimed anti-bullying program, to a combined audience of more than 500,000 students, teachers, and parents nationwide at the behest of such entities as the United States Department of the Interior, the United States Department of Justice, the National Catholic Educational Association, the American School Counselor Association, the Illinois Association of School Boards, and countless local school districts, many of whom are adopting her initiatives as part of their core bullying prevention curriculum. *It's NOT Just Joking Around!* has also generated hundreds of thousands of dollars in grant awards for schools and organizations coast to coast.

Blanco has successfully intervened in numerous bullying-related attempted suicides and acts of student retaliation. She is a respected crisis-management consultant and expert witness in the areas of school violence and peer abuse and is frequently called upon by the media as an expert interview. Some of the outlets who have turned to her for commentary include *Newsweek*, *USA Today* (two front-page stories), CBS, NBC, FOX, CNN, *Anderson Cooper 360°*, and National Public Radio. She has been a frequent guest on bullying-related breaking stories for HLN's *News Now*, with Mike Galanos, *Issues with Jane Velez-Mitchell*, and *Nancy Grace*, among many other of the nation's top news shows. Blanco has bylined multiple articles for CNN.com (front page) and the *Huffington Post*, was the focus of an in-depth front-page Q and A on Oprah.com, and her life story has been featured on *CBS Evening News*, in *Parade*, *Teen Newsweek*, *USA Today*, *Guideposts for Teens*, *Hispanic* magazine, the *Chicago Tribune*, and hundreds of local daily papers worldwide.

Blanco's work has been published in Japanese, Chinese, Danish, Lithuanian, Indonesian, and Arabic. She lives in Florida. For more information on Blanco and how to bring her to your school or community to share her story live, visit her website at *www.jodeeblanco.com*.